PRESENT YOURSELF

W9-AVW-456

also by Michael Gelb

Body Learning: An Introduction to the
Alexander Technique

PRESENT YOURSELF

THE SIMPLE WAY TO GIVE POWERFUL
AND EFFECTIVE PRESENTATIONS

Michael Gelb

AURUM PRESS

Copyright © Michael Gelb 1988

First published 1988 by Aurum Press Limited,
33 Museum Street, London WC1A 1LD

Illustrations by Willow

All rights reserved. No part of this book may be
reproduced or utilized in any form or by any means,
electronic or mechanical, including photocopying,
recording or by any information storage and retrieval
system, without permission in writing from
Aurum Press Ltd.

ISBN 0 948149 91 4
0 948149 98 1 (pbk)

Typeset by Bookworm Typesetting, Manchester
Printed in Great Britain by The Bath Press, Avon

This book is dedicated to Tony Buzan

Contents

Acknowledgements

Many thanks to the following people who have contributed to the creation of this book: Ann Darby Hutchinson, Beret Arcaya, Ed Bassett, the Gelbs (especially Joan) and the Kendalls, Shelley Liebman, Suzanne Nelson, Vanda North, Mike Rozek, Carla Siegel, Susan Southard, Ake Wilsby, Brad Winch, Ellen Wingard and Connie Zweig.

And special thanks to:

Leslie Traub, whose creativity, editorial expertise, feedback, love and support were essential to the creation of this book;

Tony Buzan, creator of Mind-Mapping, renaissance man and endless source of inspiration; and

Nancy Margulies, all-round creative genius.

Foreword

BY TONY BUZAN

Once in a while a new book appears which transforms the way we look at a familiar subject.

The subject is presentation skills.

The book is *Present Yourself* by Michael J. Gelb.

In business, in education and throughout the professions, presentation skills have become essential to advancement. The book you now hold in your hand provides you with a unique and original perspective on developing those skills.

Present Yourself is the first book on presentation skills to be brain-based, considering in detail the brain-needs of the presenter and the brain-needs of the audience. In this way, the author has captured the essential elements necessary to any communicator, while at the same time considering the needs of every listener.

Present Yourself is the first book on presentation skills to combine the pioneering work of F. Matthias Alexander on appropriate body use, with my own work on the nature of creativity, memory, thinking and the new method of accessing your own intelligences, Mind Mapping.

It is also the first book on presentation skills that provides you with information on how to present while simultaneously offering an ongoing programme of self-development.

In the true sense of the word 'liberation', Michael Gelb provides you with information that allows you an easy, step-by-step process to liberate your natural charisma; to discover the true communicator, the true genius, the *actual* you.

As the book is unique, so is Michael Gelb uniquely qualified to write it. He has lectured and presented throughout the world to audiences of all sizes (from one to 250,000) and all levels (from the severely brain-damaged and disadvantaged to the highest levels of academia), and to those practising in all the major areas of business, education and the professions. His clarity of expression, physical poise, energy, humour and compassion enable him to captivate all kinds of audiences at all levels.

I have personally had the delight of experiencing Michael's ability to deal with circumstances which are the standard nightmares for any communicator. In giant lecture halls, with a few minutes to go before commencement, the lights have gone out, audio-visual, sound systems and air-conditioning have broken down, chairs and desks have collapsed under participants, fire bells and bomb scares have interrupted, last-minute changes have been requested, coffee has been spilled on his lecture materials ...

Not once did I see him falter. Not once did he fail to handle the situation with poise and humour, turning imminent disaster into inevitable success.

Indeed, when you read *Present Yourself*, you will be reading a book, to recoin a familiar phrase, by a preacher who practises what he preaches about the practice of preaching!

In reading the book, you will actually feel as if you are part of one of the presentations for which the author is so renowned.

My own international lecturing career was profoundly and positively affected by Michael helping me to apply to my own presentations many of the principles expressed in this book, particularly those which relate to his interpretation of the work of F. Matthias Alexander. Working with Michael has allowed me to communicate my own thoughts more completely and effortlessly to my audiences.

One of the hallmarks of a commitment to excellence in any discipline is a never-ending search for accurate and objective feedback regarding one's performance. Over the twelve-year period that Michael and I have worked together, we have provided each other with critical information regarding our respective performances. Cooperating in this way, we have discovered insights that challenged us to explore new levels of presentational power. This approach to giving and receiving feedback – about which you will shortly be reading – is inspirational and invaluable.

When I first started my own research into the functioning of the human brain, and subsequently developed Mind Mapping, I had a dream that others would see the same vision, and translate it into different realities.

Present Yourself is one of my dreams come true. With clarity, concision and veracity, Michael has accurately interpreted my own work and the work of others such as Roger Sperry and F. M. Alexander, applying his own exceptional creativity to stamp a new coin.

This precious book enables each one of us to gain

access to our own rich resources and to express confidently and comprehensively the wealth and depth of our own unique knowledge, questionings, beliefs and enthusiasms.

Present Yourself is for the beginner and the advanced communicator; it is for trainers, for teachers, for managers, for anyone who has to speak in front of large groups, for anyone speaking to the smallest of groups.

It is for you.

It will become the standard work in its field.

Introduction

Think about the last presentation you attended. Was it fascinating? Engaging? Highly informative? How much of it do you remember?

The average presentation is boring and easily forgotten. Boring, because fear causes people to limit their natural expressiveness and seek refuge in mediocrity. Easily forgotten, because presentations are usually designed and delivered in a fashion which ignores the most fundamental organ of human communication – the brain.

The human brain is the most magnificent instrument in the world: more complex and powerful than the greatest supercomputers. Yet ninety-five per cent of what we know about the brain has been discovered in the last ten years.[1] We are only beginning to learn how to apply this knowledge to improving human memory, learning and communication. We have discovered that our brains have evolved over millions of years to help us learn effectively and communicate with one another. Every healthy baby is born with a tremendous capacity for vibrant and expressive communication, but all too often that natural capacity is stifled by a system of schooling which instils an exaggerated fear of making mistakes.

Freedom from fear and a practical understanding of the workings of the brain are essential ingredients for high performance presentations.

Present Yourself goes right to the heart of these two issues. In the chapters which follow, you will learn about the brain's complexity and its potential as the centre of all communication, and thus the essential key to presentation skills. We will consider the popular notion of left-brain/right-brain, and its implications for giving well-organized, creative presentations.

You will be introduced to 'Mind Mapping' - a revolutionary alternative to outlining, which gives you access to your brain's unlimited potential for creativity. This technique will help you generate ideas for your presentations faster and with greater flexibility. It will enhance your ability to organize and remember your material, while encouraging more spontaneity and originality in your delivery.

You will also learn a number of simple, effective strategies for rehearsing and mastering your material, including how to programme your brain for success every time you make a presentation by using positive visualization.

As well as learning about the practical workings of your own brain, you will also gain major insights into the brains of your audience. You will discover how to think about your audience and anticipate their needs. This is simple common sense, the importance of which cannot be over-emphasized.

You will be given eight specific keys to making the content and timing of a presentation 'brain-friendly', and therefore engaging and unforgettable. You will learn how to create a brain-nourishing environment, considering everything from lighting and ventilation to your appearance and audio-visual aids; and how each of these elements can have a profound effect on your audience's ability to understand and retain what you say.

Understanding your brain and the brains of your audience will build your confidence and make you a better speaker. But in order to be a superior presenter – to be the best you can be – you must also learn to recognize and transform the energy of fear. Fear is a universal phenomenon experienced by every speaker. According to a recent poll, public speaking is the number one fear of almost half the population.[2] Most people who have addressed a group will have experienced nervousness, stiffness and uncertainty. Fear often causes speakers to focus on *surviving* their presentations with a minimum of risk. As a result, they deliver unimaginative and mechanistic speeches, paralysing their natural self-expression and anaesthetizing their audience.

This book is based on the ideas that everyone is capable of doing much more than merely surviving a presentation, and that speaking to a group can be a stimulating, fulfilling and enjoyable experience. It deals with the issue of fear head-on. You will gain an understanding of the subtle mechanisms of fear, so that you can control your reaction to it before it interferes with your performance. You will learn how to take the energy that fear provides and turn it to your advantage. And you will be introduced to powerful methods for developing fear-free, articulate body language, including some of the trade secrets of the theatrical profession, all of which will greatly enhance the impact of every presentation you give.

It is a common belief that people are either inherently comfortable and effective in front of groups, or they are not. *Present Yourself* is based on the conviction, born of years of experience, that everyone is capable of learning how to give a superior presentation. *You already have every basic tool you need to become a superior presenter.* All you need is to find out how to make the most of those tools. You don't need to try to be something you are not. You don't need to be afraid. You don't need to be slick. You merely need to apply some simple common sense and start presenting what you already have to give – honestly, intelligently, sensitively and powerfully.

Through my company, High Performance Learning, based in Washington, DC, I have led seminars for people from all walks of life, from senior executives and other employees of IBM, DuPont, General Motors, AT&T and many other corporations, to the US Army, the National Guard, police departments, government offices, schools and hospitals. They have ranged from neophytes or presentation-phobics to experienced trainers and top-level professional speakers.

The richest experience I have in my work is watching people, whatever their level, discover how enjoyable it is to stand in front of a group, without fear, pretence or unnecessary effort, and give the very best of themselves to an audience. And then to hear them say, 'Why didn't anyone ever tell me that this could be so much fun!'

As you read this book, I wish this joy to you.

Michael J. Gelb
Washington, DC, 1987

CHAPTER 1

Meet your brain

An interest in the brain requires no justification other than a curiosity to know why we are here, what we are doing here, and where we are going. Dr Paul MacLean, Director of the Laboratory of Brain Evolution and Behavior, National Institute of Mental Health.

Our educational system, and modern society generally, discriminate against one whole half of the brain. In our present educational system, the attention given to the right hemisphere is minimal, compared to the training lavished on the left side. Roger Sperry, Nobel Laureate in physiology and medicine

Your brain is a remarkable instrument. Right now, as you read this page, it is making 100,000 chemical reactions per second. Its 12 billion neurons have the potential to make more patterns of connection than the number of atoms estimated to exist in the universe. The neural circuitry of your brain is at least 1400 times more complex than the entire world telephone system.[3]

A great deal of evidence suggests that our brains store the memory of everything we have ever seen, heard, touched, smelled or thought. Its capacity appears to be unlimited.[4] Yet this vast capacity lies largely dormant because the majority of us have never learned how to use our brains to the full. Psychologists estimate that we tap less than one per cent of our brain's potential.[5]

Why? Most of us haven't 'met' our brains. In school, we are taught arithmetic, history and science, but we are not taught about the brain and its unlimited possibilities. Very few of us come to appreciate the brain and its fundamental relationship to creativity, learning, memory and communication – or to making presentations.

ALL PRESENTATIONS ARE BRAIN-BASED

Consider what happens during a presentation. A presenter's brain 'talks' to the brains of the audience members, just as my brain is generating these words for your brain, through your eyes, to read. All communication is 'brain-to-brain' communication.

Yet if you have ever read a book or attended a course on presentation skills or public speaking, you probably didn't even hear the brain mentioned. And whether you are a veteran presenter or a beginner, you have probably never prepared a presentation from a 'brain-based' perspective. Without such a perspective, you run the risk of using only half your brain, and having only half the impact you could have on your audience. Let me explain.

'LEFT-BRAIN' BIAS

In the early 1970s Dr Roger Sperry, a Nobel Laureate in physiology and medicine, did pioneering research which led to the popular notion of 'left-brain' and 'right-brain' thinking.

By studying the brain waves of people engaged in learning different kinds of tasks, Sperry and his colleagues concluded that each of the brain's two hemispheres – or sides – tend to specialize in certain kinds of thought. The left hemisphere was found to be primarily responsible for processing logic, language, details, mathematical reasoning and analysis, while the right side deals with rhythm, colour, spatial relationships, imagination and synthesis.[6]

Unfortunately, our education grooms us from an early age to overemphasize 'left-brain' activities. Reading, writing and arithmetic – the three R's – are the first three subjects most of us study. Those who excel in these 'left-brain'dominant skills are considered 'brainy', and most likely to succeed.

On the other hand, those children who excel in creative doodling, day-dreaming and drumming innovative rhythms on their desks are viewed in a different light. These expressive, imaginative children are often labelled as 'behavioural problems'. 'Right-brain' characteristics such as creativity, imagination and humour are rarely encouraged in the process of schooling.

After school we enter the workplace, where organization and efficiency are often rewarded at the expense of imagination and creativity. As a result, most of us will approach our presentations with a limiting 'left-brain' bias.

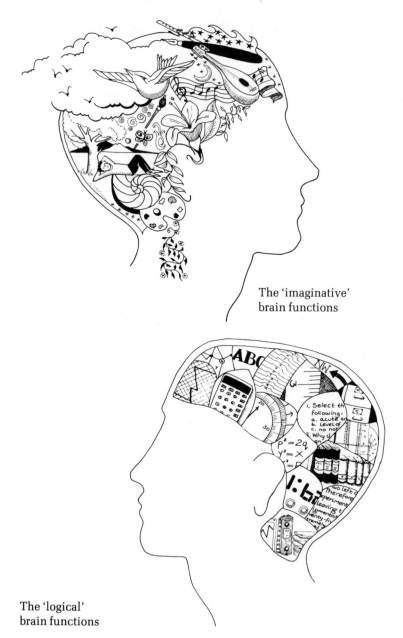

The 'imaginative'
brain functions

The 'logical'
brain functions

WHOLE-BRAINED PRESENTATIONS

Intelligent people – business men and women, teachers and others – will often assemble a factual presentation, offer it in a step-by-step fashion, concentrating on detail, and assume that it will be well received. But while a presentation must of course be based on informative, well-organized material, it needs other facets to make it compelling, such as variation in pacing, articulate body language, and plenty of vivid verbal and visual imagery.

Why? Researchers have found that the brains of audience members tend to focus on the body language, rhythm and imagery of the speakers more than on the words they say. These 'right-hemisphere' elements are more arresting than the words themselves.[7]

It follows, therefore, that if you are to make your presentation engaging and memorable, you must use your whole brain – integrating imagery and intuition with logic and analysis.

SUMMARY

In order to give a powerful presentation you must meet your brain, your whole brain, because only by using both its 'sides' – the logical and the imaginative – will you be able to communicate fully with the brains of your audience.

You may wonder how you can start using both sides of your brain. In the next chapter I wish to show you a whole-brain technique for generating and organizing ideas for your presentations. You will be astonished at what your brain, the same one you have been carrying around with you all these years, can do.

9

CHAPTER 2

Map your mind

Mind Mapping is to the information and space ages what outlining was to the medieval and industrial ages.   Tony Buzan

Chris, a manager at a large corporation, regularly gives speeches and presentations. For many years he found this to be an almost unbearably difficult undertaking. His main problem was his difficulty over generating and organizing ideas. Although he was very knowledgeable in his subject, he often found that when he sat down to prepare a speech, his mind would go blank.

Like most of us, Chris was trained to generate and organize his thoughts using an outline. As we all know, an outline begins with Roman numeral I. Chris would sit at his desk for long periods of time waiting for Idea Number I. After what seemed like an eternity, he would get his idea, and move on from there.

He would often find that when he got down to, say, III C, it should really be II A. He would start crossing out and drawing arrows, and suddenly realize that his neat outline had become a mess. Sometimes at this point he would begin doodling or day-dreaming; at other times he would just crumple his paper in frustration and start again. Over the years, he has filled many a wastepaper-basket to overflowing.

THE TROUBLE WITH OUTLINING

Chris is not alone. My research shows that the average executive spends the equivalent of three days preparing a forty-five minute presentation – a period full of frustration, discarded ideas and crumpled up pieces of paper.

Usually, when we try to generate and organize thoughts for a presentation, we waste a lot of time and energy waiting for our good ideas to emerge. The only tool we are ever given to help us generate ideas is the time-honoured system of outlining. But this method actually slows our thinking and limits our creativity.

Why? Because outlining imposes order *prematurely* on the process of thinking, thereby interfering with the speed and range of our idea generation. It is a lopsidedly 'left-brained' technique.

Our brains possess an unlimited potential for idea generation, but they work best when we allow our ideas to flow freely *before* attempting to organize them. So when we force a confining, half-brained system such as outlining on our flowing, active whole-brain, we slow down its productivity – and all too often, wrench it to a halt. Then it can't generate ideas effectively.

We also require a high degree of logical thinking in order to plan a compelling, organized sequence for our presentations. Without organization, creativity is stillborn.

11

Ideally, we need a hybrid alternative to outlining: a technique that is sufficiently 'right-brain' oriented to help our minds create ideas freely, yet allows the 'left brain' to play its part in ensuring order and attention to detail.

Enter Mind Mapping.

INTRODUCING MIND MAPPING

Mind Mapping was developed in the early 1970s by the British writer and brain researcher Tony Buzan, as a whole-brain alternative to outlining. The technique makes it easier to come up with ideas, while also enhancing the ability to organize them. It allows the analytical, detail-oriented left side to work in harmony with the more imaginative right.[8]

Using a Mind Map enables you to represent your ideas using key words, colours and imagery. Its non-linear format encourages the spontaneous generation of ideas, and allows you to put a tremendous amount of significant information on one piece of paper.

There are seven guidelines to effective Mind Mapping.

1. Start your map by drawing a picture of your topic in the centre of your paper. This drawing will serve as the home base for your creative associations. Pictures help to 'jump-start' the right hemisphere of your brain. They are much easier to remember than words and, strange as it may seem, will enhance your ability to think creatively about your subject. Don't worry if you think you can't draw, just get your image down on paper. You will still get the 'brain benefits', whatever the drawing is like.[9]

2. Use key words. Key words are rich in information.

Central image

Key words

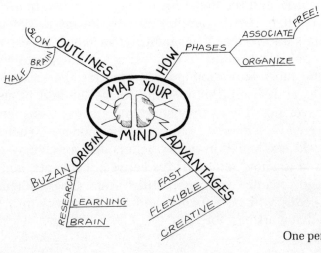

One per line

They are the 'nuggets' of recall and creative association. Key words can be generated faster than the complete sentences used in outlines, without sacrificing meaning.[10] They are also easier to remember than sentences.

3. Connect the key words with lines radiating out from your central image. By linking words with lines, you will show clearly how one key word relates to another. Connect the lines for maximum clarity.

4. Print your key words. The printed word is much easier to read and remember.

5. Print one key word per line. By printing just one word per line, you minimize clutter and leave yourself free to find the maximum number of creative associations for each word. Occasionally you may feel compelled to print a phrase or sentence, but it is best if possible to maintain the discipline of one word per line.

6. Use colours, pictures and codes for emphasis. Important points and relationships between different branches of your map can be emphasized by means of colours, pictures and codes. You might, for instance, order your main points by colour-coding, using a yellow highlighter for the most important points, blue for the secondary points, and so on. Pictures and images should be used wherever possible as they stimulate creative association and greatly enhance your memory. Codes – such as asterisks, exclamation marks, letters and numbers – can be used to show relationships between concepts, and as tools to organize your map still further. These pictures and codes will be personal and idiosyncratic; find the ones that work best for you.

Colours, pictures, codes

7. Free-associate, then organize. The process of making a Mind Map to prepare a speech or presentation is divided into two major phases.

a. The first focuses on generating as many ideas in as short a time as possible. In this *free association phase*, simply let your mind go and print as many key words and images as you can summon up. Even if a word seems ridiculous or irrelevant, put it down and keep the process

15

flowing. In so doing, you will be surprised to see how easy it is to get access to all that you know on the given subject. You will also enjoy discovering how seemingly irrelevant associations can lead to new creative insights.

b. After your brain has generated a wealth of associations, you will begin the second part of the process: *the organization phase.* Here, you will examine your map from a more analytical perspective, eliminating those elements that now seem superfluous and consolidating your key concepts. You can use numbers, additional colours, letters or other codes to impose a clear sequence on your material. In some instances, you may wish to redo your map in order to organize it further. At this stage you might, for example, put your first point at one o'clock and proceed accordingly in a clockwise rotation. You may even choose to translate the map into outline form.

MIND MAPPING YOUR PRESENTATION

Mind Mapping is very easy. It doesn't demand much – just your brain, a few coloured pens, a piece of paper and a willingness to learn something new.

Try making a Mind Map to help you prepare for your next presentation. Or if you just want to experiment with Mind Mapping, make up a topic. Either way, use the following points to guide you.

- To begin, get a large sheet of plain paper – preferably white, and the bigger the better – and five or more coloured pens. Phosphorescent highlighters are also useful, since you can read through them. (One pen and a small sheet of paper will still work at a pinch, however.) Place the paper horizontally on a table or desk in front of you.

- Having identified the topic for your presentation, draw an image which represents it in the middle of the paper. It doesn't matter what the image is, whether it is abstract or concrete, as long as it reminds you of your topic. Draw it as vividly as you can, using at least three different colours. Have fun, and don't worry about the accuracy of your drawing. (Remember guideline no. 1.)

- Next, look at your sketch and start printing key words on lines radiating out from your central image. Remember to print on the lines, one key word at a time, and keep the lines connected (guidelines 2–5). Use pictures and colours whenever possible (guideline 6). Let your associations occur spontaneously (guideline 7a), and fill the page as quickly as you can. If you run out of room and the ideas are still flowing, get another piece of paper and keep going. If you get stuck, choose any key word on your map and immediately print your first association with that word – even if it seems totally irrelevant. Keep your associations flowing, and don't worry about making sure that every word is 'right'.

- When you feel you have generated enough material, take a look at the result: all the ideas for your presentation spread across one page. Having given your right-brain the spotlight as the generator of these ideas, shift focus and use your left-brain to put your map in order.

- As you look at your map in this more analytical way, you will begin to see relationships which will help you to organize and harmonize the presentation you are planning. Look for words that recur throughout your Mind Map. They often suggest the major themes that will integrate the different aspects of your talk.

- Connect related parts of your map with arrows, more lines, codes and colours – whatever works best for you. Eliminate anything that now seems extraneous. Pare your map down to the ideas you need for what you're going to say. Then put them in sequence. If necessary, redo the map to make it neater and easier to follow (guideline 7b).

THE ADVANTAGES OF MIND MAPPING

As you experiment with Mind Mapping, its advantages in comparison to outlining will become increasingly obvious.

Mind Mapping gives you easier access to your brain's potential. It allows you to get started quickly, and to generate more ideas in less time. Its free-ranging format – adding words to one branch of your map one moment, then skipping over to another branch the next – increases your chances of generating new material.

Mind Mapping activates your whole brain. It lets you develop a logical sequence and detailed organization of your material, while encouraging imagination and spontaneity.

Mind Mapping enables you to represent a tremendous amount of information in a relatively small space. You can have all your notes for a presentation on one piece of paper, with your ideas arranged in a way that encourages you to see relationships between them. Mind Mapping gives you a clear view of *both the details and the whole picture* of your presentation.

Mind Mapping makes memorizing your presentation much easier. Colours, images and key words, the three central ingredients of Mind Maps, are much more engaging to the brain than sentences. A well-made Mind Map is almost impossible to forget. (See Chapter 5 for information on using a Mind Map as a tool for memorizing your speech.)

Most importantly, Mind Mapping is more fun than outlining. It encourages creativity and humour in the process of developing a presentation. This in turn leads to a more lively and engaging delivery.

SUMMARY

If you have done your first Mind Map as a result of
reading this chapter, you now have a better idea of what
your brain – your whole-brain – can produce. Through
Mind Mapping, you can start to infuse your presentations
with more life, creativity and fun.

Yet no matter how good you become at generating and
organizing ideas, your presentation must be designed
with the brains of your audience in mind. In the end, all
that counts is what your audience gets.

In the next chapter, you will find methods for ensuring
that your audience gets your message.

CHAPTER 3

Think of them

The meaning of communication is the response that it elicits. R. Bandler and J. Grinder, *Frogs into Princes*

A few years ago I was scheduled to speak at a telephone company conference. The speaker who preceded me on the programme was reputed to be one of the world's leading experts on the technology of communication. He gave what sounded like a tremendously authoritative speech, most of which was too technical for me to understand. As it turned out, most of those attending the conference didn't understand it either.

Knowing something well and being able to communicate it effectively to an audience are two very different things. Even an expert on the technology of communication is not necessarily an expert at communicating.

Ultimately, the success of any presentation can only be measured from the audience's perspective. Although this is simple common sense, many of us get so caught up in our own subject, or our own nervousness, that we forget to think about the audience. In order to give a powerful, effective presentation, it is essential to think about more than just yourself and your material – you must also consider your audience. In other words, since all communication is 'brain-to-brain', we can't give effective presentations without focusing on the brains of our audience.

Many speakers make the mistake of assuming that their listeners will be like empty sponges, passively soaking up their remarks. Years of sitting in classrooms often conditions us to this standard of communication. It becomes all too easy to forget the audience, and to have them forget you.

If you consider how you yourself react when you are part of an audience, you will realize how much the success or failure of a presentation depends on taking the listeners' perspective into account. It is essential that you do not allow involvement with your material to overwhelm your awareness of the audience. Like the communications expert referred to earlier, many speakers become so enamoured with their subject that they ignore their audience entirely.

Having extensive knowledge of a subject in no way ensures that you will be able to communicate effectively. Your knowledge remains dormant unless your presentation is directed, from the beginning, to the brains of the audience.

KNOW YOUR AUDIENCE

In order to know your audience, you must put yourself in their position. You will be better able to do this if you can answer the following questions about the composition, nature and mood of your audience:

What are they expecting?
What do they want to know?
Are they attending voluntarily?
How many people will be attending?
What is the age and gender distribution of the group?
What are their cultural/religious orientations?
Do they speak a particular jargon?
Are decision-makers present? Who are they?
Will the audience be feeling energetic, enthusiastic, relaxed, tired, irritable or hostile?
What activities will precede or follow my presentation –other presentations? Cocktails? Meals?
In sum, with what expectations or prejudices will the brains of the audience be filled as they prepare to listen to me?

By applying what you have learned from these questions to the design of your presentation, you will be much more likely to achieve a working rapport with the audience. And a rapport provides the essential context for successful communication.

INTELLIGENCE GATHERING

To be able to answer the questions listed above, you must take every opportunity to obtain information about the audience before you make your presentation. Here are some simple ways to gather this 'intelligence'.

Start by questioning the person who invited you to make the presentation. Many people are afraid that they will be perceived as nosy or rude for asking questions. On the contrary, experience shows that your thoroughness and interest will be appreciated.

Then speak to anyone you can who is familiar with the group you will be addressing. It is especially valuable to interview speakers who have addressed the audience previously.

In the meantime, read anything that might give you useful information about your audience, such as annual reports, company publications or newspaper and magazine articles.

One of my favourite techniques for getting to know the audience is to arrive early and make informal contact with a few of the participants. I can often find out a great deal about the mood and expectations of the group by initiating friendly conversation. This allows me to discover any potential problems, and address the immediate concerns of the audience. In one instance, twenty minutes before beginning a two-day seminar I discovered through an informal conversation that one-third of the participants had just been told that they might be laid off from their jobs. With the help of a quick Mind Mapping session, I altered my design accordingly, and made the most of a potentially disastrous situation.

Another time, I had prepared a speech for a client with whom I hadn't worked in over seven years. The speech was to be given at the end of a conference to five hundred senior managers from around the world. I was not able to get a clear idea of how to focus my speech from discussions with the people who invited me, and other sources were not readily available. I planned my speech based on what I had known about the group seven years ago, but decided to travel to the conference site the evening before in order to gather 'intelligence' from the participants. There I discovered that the group had changed dramatically, and realized that the focus of my speech was now inappropriate. I altered my design, and began by talking about the changes I had observed. The audience knew immediately that I was speaking to them, and this rapport created the context for success.

Whether you are leading a seminar, addressing a group of five hundred or talking to your local PTA, it is critically important to know your audience, and to *think of them*.

SET YOUR OBJECTIVES

Having thoroughly considered your audience, you must decide what you want them to know and to do as result of your presentation.

Setting your objectives carefully is a matter of common sense. Yet it is amazing to discover how rarely this is done. All too often presentations are approached with fuzzy intentions. Failure to set clear objectives is a hallmark of mediocrity. Choosing your objectives consciously is a critical key to high performance.

Start by generating your objectives through Mind Mapping. Then write them down in complete sentences, as this will enable you to hone your objectives further. For example, if you were giving a sales presentation you might write the following: 'At the end of this presentation, my audience will know the three major reasons why my product is superior to the competition's, and they will buy it.' Or if you are a teacher giving a lecture you might write this: 'All my students will leave this lecture knowing the seven major reasons for the French Revolution, so that they will be able to use that information to excel in next week's test.'

To better focus your objectives, try the following

approach: imagine each member of the audience being interviewed by the national news media immediately after your presentation. Envisage them being asked, 'What did you learn in this presentation?' and 'What will you do differently as a result of this presentation?' Further imagine them answering confidently in terms of your objectives for them. By focusing your objectives in this way, you will clarify what will be communicated brain-to-brain, thereby sharpening your impact.

SUMMARY

In this chapter I have emphasized the importance of knowing your audience and applying this knowledge in every presentation. I have also highlighted the necessity of setting specific objectives for every presentation you give – objectives that take into account what you want your audience to know and do as a result of your presentation.

Always remember that the success of your presentation is ultimately measured in terms of what the audience receives. *It's what your audience gets that counts.*

In the next chapter I will take this idea a step further, by showing you how an audience remembers. Through developing a deeper understanding of the brains of your audience, you can virtually guarantee that they will remember everything you wish them to.

CHAPTER 4

Build their recall

Understanding is not the same as remembering.
Tony Buzan

If you are engaged in preparing a presentation in the manner I have been suggesting, you may be feeling a certain excitement – a sense that your presentation is going to be far better than any you have ever given.

It will be!

Yet in order for it to be truly successful, you must make sure that your audience *remembers* it.

Before you continue, please try the following simple memory exercise. On the next page are forty words. Read through them once only, left to right. Don't study them. Read each word to yourself, taking no more than sixty seconds to read them all. Then cover the page.

Now make a note of the words you remember, and ask yourself why you remembered those particular words.

FORTY-WORD MEMORY EXERCISE

car   deck   table   tree   snow   bottle

money   dog   pole   sand   sky   dog

plant   book   soap   spoon   music   plant

rug   Groucho   Marx   plant   cellar   gate

pillow   dog   presentation   skills   trunk   paper

road   knife   stool   hay   smile   string

plant   wheel   air   expert   rain   bird

This exercise highlights the way in which memory works during a period of learning. Most people are more likely to remember the first few words – *car, deck, table* – and the last few words on the list – *air, expert, bird* – than they are the words in the middle. Exceptions include words which are repeated – *plant* and *dog* – words which are unusual – *Groucho Marx* – or those with special personal meaning in their context – *presentation skills*.

YOUR AUDIENCE'S MEMORY

Along the same lines, studies show that when people attend a presentation, they recall certain parts of it more vividly than others.[11]

Specifically, their brains lock on to a presentation's beginning (the primacy effect) and end (the recency effect), and any of its elements that are unusual, repeated over and over, or personally involving.

How can you help your audience remember your presentation? Simple ... by applying an understanding of how recall functions over time to the design and delivery of your material.

THE FIVE KEYS TO AUDIENCE RECALL

If you want your presentation to be memorable, you must keep the following five points in mind as you develop and deliver your presentation. *Begin powerfully* – emphasize the main points in the beginning of your talk; *repeat regularly* – review your key points throughout; *Emphasize unusually* – make your key points in humorous, outstanding or unusual ways; *Maximize involvement* – create plenty of opportunities for the audience to get involved with your presentation, and *end powerfully* – emphasize your main points again at the end: finish with a bang!

Now let's go into each of these ideas in more detail.

Begin powerfully. There are two major components necessary for taking advantage of the primacy effect.

a. *Make contact*. Start by making contact with your audience while focusing on your objectives. The best way to do this is to 'zero-in' from the beginning on what you want your audience to get from the presentation. *Wanting to communicate* with your audience is the key to making contact with them. This attitude will come through in your eyes, your posture, and the way you move. It is more important than any ice-breaking gimmick. Having said that, there are a number of useful ways to get things rolling. You can begin by asking your audience a question (real or rhetorical), you can tell a joke or a story, initiate a discussion, offer an exercise or a challenge, use audio-visuals, even act out a skit.

I recommend that you avoid using any kind of 'canned' introduction. Use your creativity to make up your own opening. Whatever technique you use to break the ice, make sure that it is related to what you want the audience to remember. For example, if I were giving a presentation on 'Making Your Presentations Unforgettable', I might use the forty-word memory test (see page 29) as an opening.

b. *Give the audience an overview.* Research shows that an audience responds positively to being given a sense of the 'shape' of a presentation.[12] The preacher's proverbial advice, 'Tell'em what you're gonna tell'em', is sound. Let the people know where you are taking them, and how you are going to get them there. For example, in my speech on 'Making Your Presentations Unforgettable' I might follow my forty-word ice-breaker exercise by saying something like: 'In the next hour, I'm going to show you how to make your presentations unforgettable, every time. The key to giving unforgettable presentations lies in understanding how an audience's memory works. Before you leave here today, you will know the five crucial elements that make a presentation unforgettable. These five elements are ...'

Repeat regularly. Just as you were more likely to remember the words 'plant' and 'dog' in the forty-word exercise, so your audience will be better able to remember points that you repeat regularly. Commercial advertisers often follow this principle (and all the other principles outlined in this chapter) to the extreme by incessantly repeating product names or telephone numbers ('Call 979–9000, that's 979–9000. Remember, call 979–9000 . . .').

I am not suggesting that you be extreme; only effective in the manner, for example, of one of my favourite speakers of all time, Dr Martin Luther King, Jr. He drilled a powerful idea into a nation's consciousness by repeating rhythmically, 'I have a dream.'

Emphasize unusually. Emphasize your key points by making them in unusual ways. The brains of your audience seek stimulation and entertainment. Therefore, if you make your key points in an outstanding or humorous way, the audience will eagerly grasp and remember them.

A classic example of the power of this idea was provided some years ago by Nikita Khrushchev, then the Premier of the Soviet Union. While delivering a speech at the United Nations, he punctuated his statement, 'We will bury you' (directed at the United States), by pounding a shoe on the podium. The next day, newspaper headlines around the world read 'WE WILL BURY YOU' and featured extensive passages from his speech. (In fact, Khrushchev had both his shoes on at the time. His was not the act of a madman. He had borrowed an aide's shoe to make his point unforgettable.)

The idea is not to be dramatic or funny solely for the sake of being dramatic or funny, but to ensure, through your novelty, that your key points are remembered. One of the most effective presentations I have ever heard described was given at a large chemical company: when a chemist there wanted to emphasize to his audience how non-toxic a new chemical product was, he simply picked up a spoon and started eating some of it right in the middle of his presentation. This was so startling that people there still talk about it – and the point he made – ten years later.

You don't have to bang your shoe or eat chemicals to make a point, but if you want your audience to remember your message, you must find a way, within the context of your own 'comfort zone', to express your points powerfully.

You can use your posture, gestures, eye contact and voice to drive home your message (see Chapter 8, 'Let your body talk'). You can also use colourful audio-visuals, stories, skits, jokes, parables – anything that captures your audience's attention, *as long as it is related to your subject*.

And bearing in mind the points made in Chapter 1, 'Meet your brain', the elements of humour, drama and colour will help you engage the 'whole brain' of your audience.

Maximize involvement. In order to maximize your own involvement, you may wish to take a piece of paper and make a Mind Map of all the possible ways you can involve the audience in your presentation.

If you can make your audience develop a sense of personal association with your presentation – through discussion, exercises, questions (real or rhetorical), they will remember it more vividly. Did you know that asking the members of an audience a rhetorical question significantly raises their attention level?[13]

Furthermore, if you can structure your presentation so that people are able to discover the key points for themselves, they will feel even more involved, and their recall will be even greater. Remember that the root of the word 'education' is *educare*, meaning 'to draw out' (not to stuff in!). Draw your audience out whenever possible.

I try to view a presentation as an opportunity to create a context in which members of my audience can discover for themselves the things I have come to present to them. I see my role as facilitating that process – validating and elaborating on their own discoveries.

In addition to structuring your presentation as described above, you can increase audience involvement by speaking the language that your audience speaks. You will be able to do this more easily if you follow the principles of audience 'intelligence gathering' discussed in Chapter 3, 'Think of them'.

One of the great examples of the effectiveness of this approach was provided by John F. Kennedy in his famous speech at the Berlin Wall. Kennedy began his speech with a few simple words in German – 'Ich bin ein Berliner' (I am a Berliner). He practised those words for days before his trip, and won the hearts of his listeners by speaking their language, literally and figuratively. (It is also interesting to note that Kennedy used this phrase to start his speech – applying the principles of beginning powerfully *and* maximizing involvement.)

End powerfully. Think of the best play you have ever seen, the most memorable film, the greatest concert, the finest novel you have ever read. How did they end? Powerfully. Clearly.

Recall is always high at the end of a presentation, even if the audience doesn't know the end is coming. In order to take full advantage of this recency effect, it is essential to emphasize your main points again, just before you close. You have set objectives for what you want your audience to know and to do – *this is your last chance to make sure that it knows them and does them*. Once again, the preacher's advice is sound: 'Tell'em what you told'em.' Give a clear review of the points you have made (if you used a graphic for your overview, you can use it again here) and, if appropriate, issue a call to action. Your presentation will end powerfully and clearly—with a bang!

VITAL INFORMATION: TIMING AND BREAKS

There are three more vital applications of the information on audience recall: start on time, give appropriate breaks and finish on time. These may seem obvious, yet experience shows that they are often abused. They are essential ingredients for a high performance presentation. Let us look at each one in more depth.

Be prepared to start on time. As we have seen, first impressions are very powerful. If you aren't ready to start on time, you will be coming up to the plate with two strikes against you. Lateness is the ultimate negative primacy.

The truth is, most presentations don't begin on time because organizations tend to tolerate lateness. Whoever else is late, you must never be the reason for the delay. It is also important to remember that because of this lateness phenomenon, you will probably have less time to deliver your material than you expected. Plan accordingly.

Give your audience, and yourself, a break. Over the past ten years I have given thousands of presentations, lasting from twenty minutes to five days. Participants regularly comment at the end of these sessions that not only did they learn more than they usually do in the same amount of time, but they came away with more energy than when they started. More than anything else, I attribute these results to the fact that I always give my audience, and myself, regular breaks. And I give these breaks *before* they are desperately needed.

Remember the recency effect – recall rises for the last part of a session. All too often, presentations drag on for an hour and a quarter, an hour and a half, even two hours or longer. In these cases, the audience is usually shifting, itching and scratching, desperate for a break. When the break is finally called, people dash for the door – the recency effect being 'Let me out of here!'

Presenters who abuse their audience in this manner will often say that they are reluctant to give breaks because it's so difficult to get the audience back. Of course they don't want to come back, because they never know when they are going to get a break again, and thus a vicious circle is set up.

Give your audience a break before they get desperate, preferably at a high point. Call the break when they feel energized, and will return even more energized. Leave them with the positive recency effect of 'What's next?' rather than 'Let me out of here.'

Breaks are not only important as a means of regulating your audience's energy and attention, they are essential for ensuring maximum recall. Research shows overwhelmingly that beyond fifty minutes, audience recall falls sharply. Even if the audience's understanding remains high, recall declines at this point, because understanding is not the same as remembering.[14] The same research has shown that a ten minute break given at the end of a fifty minute lecture will improve the audience's recall of the material.[15]

Appropriate breaks allow the brains of an audience to process and integrate the material they are receiving. Depending upon the time of day, and the difficulty of the material, I give breaks every half hour to an hour – from thirty second stretch breaks to ten minute leave-the-room breaks.

A useful guideline for longer presentations is ten minutes of break time per hour. I recommend that you resist the temptation to go on beyond an hour, even if everything seems to be flowing nicely. Giving appropriate

The ten minute break

breaks is ultimately an art, based on developing sensitivity to your audience. The critical point is that breaks are an essential part of your presentation.

Since most presentations require that the audience should remain in focused mode of attention, the break will allow them to shift into a more relaxed state. You might, for example, encourage your audience to stretch, take a walk and, if possible, get some fresh air. It is also a good idea to play music during the breaks. These activities change the pace, and will energize and refresh both you and your audience.

By giving your audience regular breaks, you will create more opportunities for powerful primacy and recency; everything you say will make more impact, and therefore be more memorable.

Finish on time. Never continue over your allotted time. There is no surer way to spoil an otherwise successful presentation. Even if you feel that your audience would like you to continue, don't. Resist the temptation. Let people ask you questions afterwards, if necessary. It is always better to leave them wanting more.

Before you begin speaking, jot down the time you are supposed to finish. Treat your finishing time as a contract made with your audience, and arrange to have a clock in view to help you fulfil you commitment.

SUMMARY

Can you remember the five principles of audience recall without looking back at the text? How about the three essential timing points? This information is so important that I urge you to commit it to memory. If you can

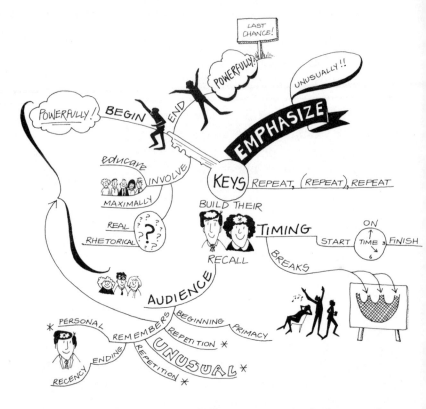

consistently begin powerfully, repeat regularly, emphasize unusually, maximize involvement and end powerfully, while giving appropriate breaks and starting and finishing on time, you will be able to guarantee an unforgettable presentation.

This chapter has emphasized the keys to building your audience's recall. In the next chapter, we are going to focus on how you can build you own recall, so that you will remember your material effortlessly and present it masterfully.

CHAPTER 5

Perfect practice

*Practice doesn't make perfect. Perfect practice
makes perfect.*   Vince Lombardi

In order to give a masterful presentation, you must be able
to remember what you want to say.

Rehearsal is the key to mastery.

Actors, musicians and athletes rehearse regularly. All
are immersed in demanding activities which involve fine
tuning, and they know that rehearsing is essential to high
performance. In the first four chapters of *Present Yourself*
we have seen that giving high performance presentations
is an equally demanding process. It is essential, therefore, to rehearse your presentations. Furthermore, the
quality of your rehearsal must be up to a certain standard
if it is to bring you maximum value.

PRACTISING PERFECTLY

How can you rehearse effectively, and tune your brain for
high performance?

The most important point is that you should begin filling your brain with positive thoughts about your presentation right from the start. When asked to do a presentation, many people will begin – consciously or unconsciously – to think negatively. In a word, they will worry. And in worrying, they will programme their brains for failure.

So instead, programme your brain for success. For example, as soon as you find that you have to do a presentation, begin visualizing yourself delivering it masterfully. Visualize, as clearly as you can, the place where the presentation will be given. Imagine yourself feeling relaxed, confident, calm and poised. View yourself moving, gesturing and speaking in an easy, fluid manner. Finally, create an image of your audience – engaged by, and involved in, your presentation.

Keep building these positive images, right through your actual presentation.

Positive, conscious visualization is one of the inner secrets of master performers in a wide range of disciplines. Athletes, actors, singers, musicians, dancers and speakers all use this powerful technique.

Your thoughts have an immediate and profound effect on the distribution of your muscle tone and the ability of your nerve impulses to fire in harmony. Research has shown that 'nourishing' your brain with positive images helps your nervous system to function at its peak. When positive visualization is practised regularly, it can significantly enhance your performance.[16]

MAKING VISUALIZATION WORK FOR YOU

Anyone can visualize successfully. In order to develop

confidence in your ability to visualize, start by seeing whether you can describe the following: a tennis ball, an ice-cream cone, a tiger, a beautiful beach, yourself. You obviously can. These images 'reside' in the occipital lobe of your brain, which stores billions of images from your own personal history. This part of your brain has the potential, at this very moment, to store an infinite series of new images, and to create an infinite number more.

There are five keys to making visualization work for you. They are: study models of excellence, relax, use multi-sensory imagination, keep the visualization positive, and practise. Let's look at how these keys apply to preparing for a presentation.

Study models of excellence. In order to gain rich material for your conscious visualization, you may find it useful to identify presenters who you consider to be models of excellence, and study them. Some of my favourites include Martin Luther King, Jr, Winston Churchill and Muhammad Ali in his prime. Find your own examples of excellence, and take every opportunity to learn from them.

Relax. Research shows that visualization exercises are more effective when practised in a relaxed state.[17] Relaxing allows your visualization to have a deeper impact. You can precede your visualization practice with a short relaxation exercise,[18] or practise visualizing as you are waking, or dozing off to sleep, as I do.

Use multi-sensory images. Use all your senses when imagining your excellent presentation. Imagine the feeling of your feet on the floor, your vision of the audience, the sounds in the room. The more vivid your imagination, the more powerful the result.

Keep your visualization positive. Imagine yourself, calm and confident, poised and powerful, flowing effortlessly through your material. Think of yourself as an excellent presenter committed to getting better and better. Research suggests that positive visualization is effective because our thoughts have the power to energize the neuro-muscular mechanisms which will perform the action.[19] When you visualize yourself doing something well, you are 'programming' your brain for success.

Practise. Reinforce your visualization of excellence regularly. By refining your visualization, you'll get better and better all the time.

Of course, visualization is most effective when combined with more traditional forms of practice. And your practice will be more effective if you can remember all your material. Before giving an overview of some simple rehearsal techniques, I would like to introduce you to a very effective way of remembering the material for your presentations.

THE MIND MAP MEMORY METHOD

Although it is fine to bring notes with you when you make your presentation, it is best to emancipate yourself from dependence upon them. You will always be better able to 'present yourself' if you work from memory. If you have used a Mind Map to prepare your presentation, you are already one step ahead.

Imagery, colour and key words make Mind Maps easy to remember, and with a little practice you will find them almost impossible to forget. Start by making a clear, comprehensive and vivid Mind Map. Then, in order to make sure that you remember it, take out a new sheet of paper and re-create the map from memory. When you have finished, check against the original map, and fill in anything you may have left out. You will find that if you follow this re-creation process two or three times, the material will be almost unforgettable. To enhance your memory further, pin the map to a wall, close your eyes, and practise re-creating it in your mind's eye. Open your eyes, and check against the original. Do this until you can re-create the entire map effortlessly. Two or three times should be sufficient.

STRATEGIES FOR REHEARSAL

In addition to the Mind Map Memory Method there are a number of other valuable rehearsal strategies, all of which will help you perform at your best. Experiment with the following, and use those which work best for you.

- Deliver your presentation to yourself aloud. Become accustomed to the rhythm, timing and feel of your message.

- Tape record your presentation. Play the tape and listen to the quality of your voice, and the overall coherence and flow of the presentation.

- Videotape your presentation. Play the tape and observe the way your posture and gesture relate to your message, again with special attention to the overall coherence and flow of the presentation.

- Give your presentation to a friend or colleague. Do this first without asking for any feedback so you can get comfortable, then ask for constructive criticism.

- For particularly important presentations, bring together as many supportive friends or colleagues as you can, and deliver your presentation to them. Ask them to play the role of the most critical, disruptive audience they can imagine, to be 'devil's advocates' and point out any possible weakness in your material or delivery. Although this experience may be somewhat unsettling, it will prepare you ably for your actual presentation – which should be easy by comparison.

- Time your practice sessions. Become familiar with the amount of time it takes to cover your key points, and bear in mind that your actual presentation will probably take longer than it does in rehearsal. Set minimum and maximum times for each 'branch' of your presentation. Anticipate the effect of questions and interruptions on your timing, and always have more material available than you will actually need.

- Practise with any audio-visuals or props you intend to use. Become fluent in any medium you intend to employ (see Chapter 6 for more detailed advice).

I recommend that you experiment with all of the above strategies, find the rehearsal methods that suit you best, and practise them faithfully.

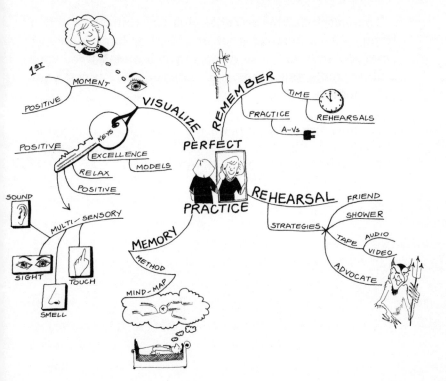

SUMMARY

The most important point of this chapter is to approach your presentation with a *positive attitude from the first moment*. You can develop this positive attitude by applying the technique of visualization. The keys to visualizing effectively are studying models of excellence, relaxing, multi-sensory imagining, keeping the images positive, and practising!.

To memorize your material, apply the Mind Map Memory Method. Re-create your Mind Map, first on paper, and then in your mind's eye.

To rehearse further, practise aloud by yourself or with a friend. Use a tape recorder or video, or have a 'devil's advocate' session. Make sure that you have mastered your audio-visuals and props, and that you have timed your presentation.

The techniques discussed in this chapter will help you to set the stage for high performance. In the next chapter, we will look at how you can literally set the stage in order to guarantee your success, still further.

CHAPTER 6

Set your stage

The medium is the message.   Marshall McLuhan

The environment in which you give a presentation has many subtle but powerful effects. The lighting, air quality, even the shape of the room, along with many other factors including your appearance and audio-visuals, can have a profound influence on your audience's ability to enjoy and remember your presentation.

A carefully constructed environment can enhance a great deal the effectiveness of your presentation, whereas the usual environment in which presentations take place tends to distract from, or vitiate, efforts to communicate effectively. For example, the average presentation is given under fluorescent lights, and there is considerable evidence that fluorescent lighting can discoordinate the two hemispheres of the brain, thereby interfering with an audience's ability to absorb information.[20] More generally, when people are uncomfortable – perhaps because their chairs are constricting, or the room is too hot – their attention level and ability to recall will suffer.

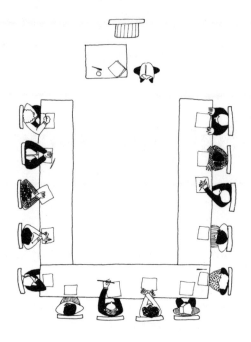

U-shape

Classroom style

With these points in mind, take an active interest in 'setting the stage' before a presentation, and, whenever possible, shape the circumstances in order to create the ideal learning environment for your audience. This will require extra preparation, but I promise that your efforts will prove worth while.

ENVIRONMENTAL FACTORS

The main factors to consider when setting your stage are:

Rooms and furniture. Always aim to give your presentation in a room that provides ample space for every member of your audience. Set up the chairs – and tables if necessary – in an arrangement most suited to the kind of presentation you are giving. For small groups of about twenty-five people or less, I find that a U-shape design is the most effective, as it encourages maximum interaction and participation. For larger groups, I prefer a modified classroom style arrangement.

Whatever seating arrangement you use, it is a good idea to remove empty chairs from the room, or at least move them to one side. Vacant seats form a 'centre of dead energy' which can unconsciously draw the audience's attention away from your message.

The important point is to set up your room and furniture in a manner which reflects concern about your audience. Consideration of this level of detail is a hallmark of excellence.

Decor. An audience seeks stimulation and involvement with its immediate surroundings. Many presentations are given in drab, generic rooms. Dull environments tend to have a dulling effect on the minds of an audience. Create an attractive, 'brain-nourishing' environment. Fresh flowers, green plants and colourful visual aids will all tend to enliven and engage your audience, thus making them more receptive to your message.

Lighting. Lighting is another important factor in a brain-nourishing environment. Unfortunately, the form of lighting available at most presentation sites – fluorescent lights – is mental 'junk food'. In addition to their disorienting effect on the brain, fluorescent lights do not cast much shadow, thereby reducing the contrast necessary for clear vision. They also often produce a low-level buzzing noise. These effects can distract your listeners, who need to see and hear you clearly in order for your remarks to have full impact. Whenever possible, make your presentations in rooms with natural or incandescent lighting.

Air and temperature. Most presentations are given in rooms with poor ventilation and temperature control. Stuffy air can lull your audience into a sleepy state, and an uncomfortable room temperature is a constant mode of distraction. You should aim to give your presentation in a well-ventilated room with a temperature of between 65 and 68°F.[21] The air quality and temperature can often be modified through the judicious opening and closing of doors and windows. If ideal temperatures cannot be met, it is better to err on the side of being too cool.

I also recommend that you maintain the quality of air in the room by asking your audience to refrain from smoking. Fresh air is already at a premium in most indoor environments, so insist that your audience only smoke outside the room during the frequent breaks you will be giving them. It is also a good idea to place five or six large green plants in the room. In addition to enlivening the environment, plants also help to freshen the air.

Your appearance. Giving thought to your appearance is another integral aspect of setting your stage. Audiences invariably react strongly to every facet of your appearance. A dragging shirt tail, mismatched colours and ill-fitting garments will all be distracting. Even the slightest quirk in your appearance is magnified in their eyes. So dress and groom yourself immaculately.

I shall refrain from giving more specific advice on how to dress, because I want to encourage you in your own personal style. I would recommend, however, that you be better dressed than your audience, especially when presenting to people senior to you. Wear clothes that fit you well, and allow for comfort and ease of movement. Find a couple of outfits that make you look and feel great. If possible wear them just for presentations. Enjoy looking your best, and let your clothes become part of your 'visualization of excellence'.

Your appearance will also be affected by the extent to which you have rested and exercised, and also by your diet. If your are a professional presenter, or if you aim to be, I recommend that you condition yourself in a manner similar to that of a professional dancer or athlete. Your general fitness, exuberance and the sparkle in your eyes are the most important aspects of your appearance.

Your introduction. The introduction is a key aspect in setting the stage for your presentation. It should affirm your credibility as a speaker, and raise the energy and attention-level of your audience. People often arrive at a presentation with their minds on the situations they have just left – from household problems to traffic jams. An effective introduction psychologically 'brings' them into the room.

Arrange to have the best speaker available to introduce you, and be prepared with a Mind Map – or outline – of what you would like him to say. Ask him to keep his introduction under two minutes, and encourage him to create an environment of expectation and interest. Be certain that all questions concerning the availability of toilets, telephones, refreshments and other basic needs are answered before the formal introduction begins.

AUDIO-VISUAL AIDS

Audio-visual aids can play a powerful role in enhancing the impact and memorability of your presentation. When used properly, they can entertain and enliven your audience while increasing their receptivity and recall.

The effective use of audio-visual equipment requires keeping in mind a few simple points.

- Remember that the primary reason for using audio-visuals is to *highlight and emphasize the key points of your presentation*. Whether you are using a flipchart, overhead projector or any other medium, do not try to fill it with detailed information. Your audience will almost always be unable to follow information presented in this way. Many presenters, instead of using a picture to represent a thousand words, like to show pictures – or slides and flipcharts – of a thousand words. Use your audio-visuals to display images, key words and phrases which summarize and highlight your main points. They will be much more effective as 'brain stimuli' for your audience.

- Don't rely on audio-visual aids to do your work for you. *You* must be the primary medium for delivering your information. Avoid hiding behind the audio-visuals, or speaking to them. Your job is not to disappear in the dark while the audience looks at slides, or to talk to your flipchart. If you do, you will lose your rapport with your audience – and the impact of your presentation will suffer.

- Only employ audio-visuals when needed. Audio-visuals are powerful tools for capturing the attention of an audience. Use them consciously. *Be certain that your audience is seeing only what you want them to see, when you want them to see it.*

- If you plan to use complex audio-visual equipment, practise with it beforehand and learn its operational ins and outs thoroughly. Nothing will be more distracting to an audience, or potentially damaging to the impact of your presentation, than you fumbling with your equipment on-stage. Always be prepared for the possibility that your equipment will fail, or that materials you requested will not be delivered.

- All visual materials should be *simple, clear, and easy to see* from all parts of the room.

Let us consider how to make the most of some commonly used visual aids.

Flipcharts. Flipcharts are readily available, portable, and easy to use. To make the most of this medium you must print legibly in large, bold letters, using different colours. Use key words or phrases, rather than sentences. Flipcharts are good for drawing diagrams, graphs and other pictures which illustrate your key points. Chart sheets should be uncluttered and easy to read. When appropriate, prepare your flipchart before your presentation.

Write on every third sheet to prevent the audience from reading through the partially transparent paper.

Only use a flipchart in a relatively small group. Sit at the back of the room before you begin your presentation to test its legibility. Flipchart sheets can be awkward to turn, making it difficult to refer to previous sheets. This can be partially overcome by using multiple charts on the same sheet.

Overhead projectors. Overhead projectors allow you to present a great deal of vivid, visual information. Projector images are easier to see than flipcharts – because they are illuminated and much larger – and therefore they can be used with groups of any size. This is a dynamic medium, which allows you to write easily while speaking. And, because you face your audience while using an overhead, it is easy to maintain contact.

I recommend that you use single sheet transparencies, because they allow you to refer quickly to previous material. Overhead projector pens come in a wide array of colours, making it easier to draw memorable images. When using the overhead for long presentations, place it on a low table so that you can sit comfortably while drawing.

Projector bulbs have a tendency to burn out at awkward moments. Always be prepared with a spare bulb (or a back-up machine). Check focus before you begin, and monitor the image on the screen regularly to be sure that it remains centred and clear.

Slide projectors. Slides can have tremendous visual clarity, impact and entertainment value. If you plan to use slides as part of your presentation, remember these few simple points: think carefully about how each slide supports your objectives, and show the minimum number of slides necessary to illuminate each of your points. Too many slides can overload your audience, and exhaust them while obscuring your message. And leaving the lights off for extended periods will often result in loss of contact with your audience.

Use a high-quality autofocus projector, and a remote-control device (or a projectionist), allowing you to move freely and interact with your audience. Always triple check to be sure that the slides are upright and in the correct order.

Video and film. Video and film can be the most engaging and entertaining audio-visual tools. They are so powerful, however, that they can often obscure the role of the presenter. They *are* the presentation, best used as a substitute for a stand-up presentation, rather than as a complement to it. So when using these media, bear in mind that you are functioning primarily as a facilitator and discussion leader.

A FEW OTHER POINTS

Handouts. Handouts are an effective way for you to provide more detailed information to your audience. If you are going to refer specifically to the handouts, distribute them first before you do so. Direct your audience to the relevant part, giving them time to read it.

When they have finished, ask them to put the handout aside.

Never distribute handouts at the beginning of the presentation, or your audience will tend to focus more on the handout than on what you have to say. If you are going to distribute handouts at the end, don't tell people as this will often lead them not to pay attention.

Music. It may not have occurred to you to add music to your presentation, but it is excellent brain food for your audience. Studies show that certain types of classical music – including the non-choral works of Beethoven, Mozart, Vivaldi and Bach – facilitate coherence between the right and left side of a listener's brain.[22] You may play this kind of music while your audience enter the room, during breaks, or as they are leaving. Using music in this way will heighten your audience's energy and receptivity while creating an aura of excellence.

Microphone. Use a microphone only when absolutely necessary. Amplified sound is often distorted and difficult to modulate properly.

It is very important when using a microphone that you should become comfortable with the amplified sound of your own voice. Always test the microphone before you begin speaking, and if you are inexperienced take some extra time to practise. If you are using a standard microphone, aim it at your mouth, from a constant distance of six to eight inches away. Whenever possible, use a cordless collar microphone to allow maximum freedom of movement, and more consistent voice modulation.

Mind Maps. You can greatly enhance the effectiveness of your presentations by using Mind Maps to communicate with your audience. Mind Mapping allows you to convey a great deal of information in a brain-compatible manner. Using Mind Maps successfully requires that you begin by giving a brief introduction of the technique. I usually tell my groups that I am going to make a simple, easy map of the ideas I will be discussing. Then, as I am speaking, I use an overhead projector and coloured pens to build a map of all my key points. As the map grows before their eyes, it creates an element of suspense which captures the audience's imagination. In addition to being easily memorable and full of information, this technique encourages high levels of attention and interest.

WHAT IF 'THEY' WONT LET ME DO IT?

In making the above recommendations I occasionally meet the objection, 'They won't let us do this,' or 'It's just not possible in the place I work.' Although there are occasions in which it is difficult to manipulate the environment in the manner I have suggested, you will be surprised at what can be accomplished if you are insistent. Whether you are giving a presentation within your own organization or coming in from the outside, you can almost always create better conditions. Ultimately, everyone will be glad that you did.

I recommend creating your own environmental checklist in preparing for presentations, and sending it, well in advance, to whoever is in charge of the arrangements. Follow up with a phone call and review each item. Arrive early enough to check the details and make any last-minute changes.

There will, of course, be times when the opportunity to create your desired environment is limited, such as when

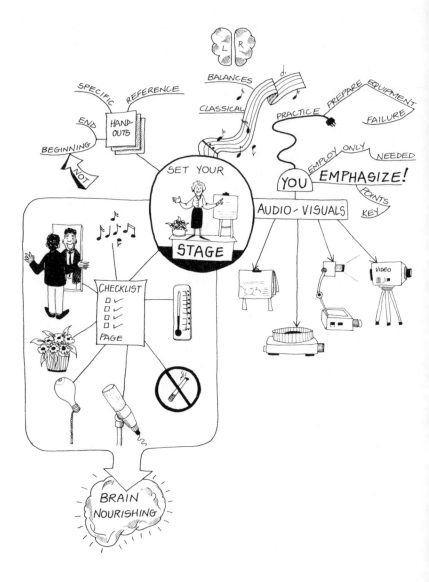

you follow other speakers at a conference. Nevertheless, you can still set your own stage, even if it means simply rearranging a table at the front of the room, bringing your own flowers, or asking that empty chairs be removed before you begin. This action shows that you care. It is a display of your self-confidence, and makes it clear that you are taking command.

SUMMARY

In this chapter, I have stressed the importance of creating a positive environment for your presentation. Thoughtful attention to what may seem like minor details – the room, ventilation and lighting, along with your appearance, introduction and use of audio-visuals – will give your presentation a distinctively superior quality.

Everything covered thus far has been designed to help you achieve a high level of self-confidence and excellence. Yet there is no greater enemy of excellence than fear. In the next chapter, I will show you how you can transform fear in order to reach your highest potential.

CHAPTER 7

Transforming fear

Fear is the mind-killer, the little death.   Frank
Herbert

For as he thinks within himself, so he is.
Proverbs 23:7

*Fear – a feeling of anxiety and agitation caused by
the presence or nearness of danger, evil, pain,
timidity, dread, terror, fright, apprehension.*
Webster's Unabridged Dictionary

What is the 'danger, evil, pain' associated with speaking
to a group? What are people afraid of when they stand
before their fellow humans?

The answer is simple. Humiliation. Embarrassment.
Loss of self-esteem and dignity.

What are the origins of this fear?

Think back to your first few years of school. Perhaps
you can recall when someone in your class enthusiasti-
cally stood up to recite, take their turn at 'show and tell',

or answer a question, and was greeted with paroxysms of mocking laughter. Both witnesses and victims of this typical scenario find that the fear of being laughed at, of being the subject of ridicule, becomes a powerful force that cripples self-expression. Some of us come away from this kind of experience with a deep dread of standing in front of a group. Most of us just learn to give boring, mediocre presentations, bereft of creativity, in order to minimize the risk of being mocked.

The most experienced speakers often feel the symptoms of fear before and during a presentation. Even a veteran actress such as Helen Hayes, with over fifty years' experience on stage, still reports feeling butterflies in her stomach prior to a show.

In this chapter I will introduce you to a practical approach towards transforming fear into power, so that the butterflies may 'fly in formation'.

The first point to understand is that there is nothing wrong with feeling fear. The key to success is knowing how to control your *reactions* to fear. When you understand how to control these reactions, you can transform the energy that fear provides into a force that helps you to be at your best.

In order to learn how to cope with fear, it is helpful to have an understanding of the mechanism through which it operates.

THE STARTLE PATTERN

During the 1960s Dr Frank Pierce Jones, a researcher at Tufts University, conducted extensive studies on the mechanism of fear. In one experiment Jones tested a group of a thousand people. He asked all of them to stand in their most comfortable posture, and then proceeded to frighten them by making a sudden noise. He found, in every case, that their reactions were the same: to tighten their neck muscles, hold their breath, and contract the major joint surfaces of their bodies. He called this profile of tension the 'startle pattern'.

Jones observed that the startle pattern provided a model for responses to any stressful situation. In other words, most people react to stressful situations by stiffening their neck muscles, holding their breath and contracting their bodies. Jones's most crucial observation was that due to the inordinate stresses of modern life, most adults become permanently trapped in a modified form of the 'startle pattern'.[23]

As a result, most people approach the act of presenting with fear already locked into their bodies. The startle pattern gradually becomes more pronounced as anxiety about an imminent presentation increases. This reaction is insidious because it usually occurs below the level of consciousness. Most people don't become aware of their reaction until they are seized by gross manifestations of fear, such as sweating palms, pounding hearts and choking throats. At this point, fear controls us.

In order to take command of fear and reach our full potential, we need to find a method for freeing ourselves from both the chronic and acute effects of the startle pattern.

THE ALEXANDER TECHNIQUE

The most effective method was developed by F. Matthias Alexander (1869–1955), an actor from Australia. Alexander's successful stage career was threatened by a persistent, stress-related tendency to lose his voice in the middle of his performances. Working on his own, Alexander observed through the use of mirrors that as soon as he began to think about reciting, he tended to tighten his neck muscles, resulting in a pulling back of his head, interference with his breathing and a shortening of his stature. He further observed that the manifestations of this pattern became more severe as he attempted to recite increasingly difficult passages. Alexander reasoned that this pattern of interference (which Jones would later call the startle pattern) was responsible for causing the problems with his voice.[24]

After long and painstaking study Alexander eventually solved his problem by developing a technique for freeing himself from this habitual pattern of constriction. As a result he became famous on the stage, renowned for his extraordinary voice and stage presence. People flocked to him for lessons, and in response to their demand he developed what came to be known as the Alexander Technique. The Alexander Technique is usually taught through a series of individual lessons in which the teacher uses a very subtle form of manual guidance to lead the pupil to an enhanced experience of balance and poise.[25] As lessons progress, the student learns to recognize and prevent unnecessary patterns of tension, thereby discovering a more graceful, integrated manner of moving and speaking.

The Alexander Technique has come to be regarded as a trade secret among professional performers, and has been taught for years at many of the world's top academies of the performing arts, including the Royal Academies of Drama and Music in London and the Julliard School of Music in New York. The Technique is an integral part of the presentation courses I provide to educators and business people around the world.

The Alexander Technique cannot be learned from a book. There is, however, one procedure drawn from Alexander's work which you can begin practising now. The procedure, which I call the Balanced Resting State, is used by Alexander teachers throughout the world. If practised regularly, it helps free you from the effects of the startle pattern. The procedure is very simple; it takes about ten minutes. Try it following the instructions below.

THE BALANCED RESTING STATE

1. Begin by placing a few books – between two and six inches in height – on the floor (preferably carpeted). Stand approximately your body's length away from the books, with your back towards them, and pause for a moment. Place your feet shoulder-width apart, keep your eyes facing straight ahead, and let your hands rest gently at your sides.

2. Think of allowing your body to lengthen and expand. You might, for example, imagine that there is a string attached to the top of your head, gently easing your head and spine up towards the ceiling. Breathing freely, become aware of the feeling of your feet on the floor and notice the distance from your feet to the top of your head. Keep your eyes focused and alive, and listen to the sounds around you.

3. Maintaining this awareness, move lightly and quickly so that you are resting on one knee. Then roll yourself back so that you are supporting yourself with your

hands behind you, feet flat on the floor and knees bent. Continue breathing easily.

4. Let your head drop forward a tiny bit to ensure that you are not tightening your neck muscles, and then gently roll your spine back along the floor so that your head is resting on the books. The books should be positioned so that they support your head at the place where your neck ends and your head begins. If your head is not well positioned on the books, reach back with one hand and support your head while using the other hand to place the books in the proper position. Add or take books away until you find what is comfortable for you. Your feet should remain flat on the floor, with your knees pointing up to the ceiling and your hands resting on the floor at your sides or loosely folded on your chest. Allow the weight of your body to be fully supported by the floor.

5. All you need in order to reap the benefit of this procedure is to rest in this position for approximately ten minutes. As you rest, gravity will be lengthening your spine and realigning your torso. Keep your eyes open to avoid dozing off. You may wish to bring your attention to your breathing and to the gentle pulsation of your whole body. Be aware of the ground supporting your back, allowing your shoulders to rest as your back widens. Let your whole body lengthen and expand. Take one or two deep breaths.

6. After you have rested for ten minutes, get up slowly, being careful to avoid tightening or contracting your body as you return to a standing position. In order to achieve this smooth transition, decide when you are going to move and then gently roll over on to your

front, maintaining your new sense of integration. Ease your way into a crawling position, and then stand lightly.

7. Pause for a moment once you have reassumed the standing posture. Again, feel your feet on the floor, and notice the distance between your feet and the top of your head. You may be surprised to discover that the distance has expanded. As you move into the activities of your day, or the presentation you are about to give, think about maintaining this sense of expansion, ease and overall 'uplift'.

For best results, practise the Balanced Resting State at least twice a day for ten minutes at a time. You can do it when you wake up in the morning, and before retiring at night. The procedure is especially valuable when you feel overworked or stressed, or when you are about to give a presentation. Regular practice will help you develop a sense of 'body confidence' – an upright, easy poise that will help you perform at your best.

WARMING UP

In addition to practising the Balanced Resting State, there is something else you can do before every presentation – warm up. This will help you transform fear and its accompanying stiffness and tension into power and poise.

All too often, speakers ready themselves for presentations like condemned prisoners approaching the walk to the gallows. They sit still and stiffen up, imagining every possible fearful eventuality. Instead of sitting and stiffening, I urge you to find a place where you can move freely, and practise as many of the following warm-up exercises as you can.

Wake up your eyes. Hold your index finger in front of your eyes and move it around, keeping your eyes focused on the tip of the finger. Move your finger at random to the limits of your visual field. Do this as quickly as you can without moving your head. Practise for thirty seconds. It works even better if you can follow the shiny tip of a pen or the beam of a pocket flashlight. This exercise will wake up your eyes. When they are alive, bright and clearly focused, so are you.

Mobilize your face. Take a minute, in front of a mirror if possible, and make as many different faces as you can: funny, sad, angry, stupid, surprised, even frightened. Exaggerate each expression, making sure that your eyes are part of it. Scrunch your face tightly, and then make as big a face as possible with your eyes and mouth wide open. Hold each face for ten seconds, relaxing for a moment in between. Do this five to ten times. Warming up your face in this manner allows you to feel more open, and permits a greater range of expression.

Breathe. While sitting in a comfortable, upright position, become aware of the flow of your breath. Follow the movement of your breathing without trying to change it for thirty seconds. Then, allow yourself a deep, full inhalation, followed by an extended, complete exhalation. Do this seven times, allowing each breath to be deeper than the one before. To enhance the effectiveness of this exercise further, make a deep, sighing 'ahhhh' sound as you exhale. This simple exercise is very powerful and relaxing. It will help you feel calm and energized at the same time.

Open your voice. Now that you are breathing freely, get your voice in gear. Experiment with yawning, sighing and humming. Sing vowel sounds in ascending and descending scales. Without straining, discover your highest and lowest notes. Sing or hum your favourite inspirational song. You can even try singing the first few minutes of your presentation. These simple voice exercises will help prevent you from choking up, as they enhance the quality and resonance of your voice.

Get your blood moving. Start by shaking your hands and feet vigorously. Then, using both hands, knead the top of your shoulders, the back of your neck and the top of your head. Follow this with a gentle massage of your forehead, temples and the orbits of each eye (being careful not to touch your eyeballs). Next massage your jaw, mush your cheeks around and pull on your ears.

Continue by using both hands to knead your legs vigorously up and down from your thighs to your ankles. Rub your abdomen in a clockwise motion, and then reach your arms behind you to massage your lower back.

You can also jog in place, juggle, dance or practise your favourite stretching exercise – whatever works best to get your blood flowing.

As you practise these warming-up exercises, you will find your fear and stiffness transformed into enthusiasm and freedom. Remember to reinforce the positive visualization of your presentation. Imagine yourself presenting in a relaxed and competent manner. Let your energy flow. What you used to call 'fear' can now be renamed excitement and anticipation.

SOME COMFORTING THOUGHTS

In addition to the practical exercises described above, a number of comforting thoughts can be useful allies in transforming fear.

Inexperienced speakers often imagine that audiences will take malicious delight in their slightest error, and, as in some vaudevillian nightmare, their first mistake will cause them to be 'hooked' off the stage to a chorus of jeers. This will not happen. Audiences are almost always extremely tolerant and sympathetic.

Always remember that *your audience wants you to succeed*. They are almost certainly attending your presentation with the hope of benefiting from it, so your success is in their best interest. Most audience members feel a natural empathy with the speaker, and will tend to be supportive if any difficulties occur.

Also, remember that *your audience is made up of individuals not unlike yourself*. There is a tendency among presenters to look upon an audience as a common mass – which, in its impersonality, seems more fearful. This tendency is exacerbated as group size increases. Whatever the size of your group, remember that it is made up of individual human beings. Never allow yourself to be intimidated by them. If you find yourself losing this perspective, look at your audience's faces and imagine what they looked like in their first-form school photographs. This is an amusing and sure-fire way of eliminating intimidation.

In addition, consider that as a presenter *you are in a situation of power and control* with respect to an audience. Enjoy it! You have been invited to take command of the moment, and if you respond to the

A light-hearted look at your audience

opportunity you will find yourself in a dynamic, power-ful position.

When you stand before a group, your sense of time is altered by the effect of adrenalin as it races through your bloodstream. Time speeds up, and it becomes all too easy to interpret your slightest nervous gesture or mis-spoken word in a grossly exaggerated manner. Your audience, however, is operating on 'normal time', and what seems a glaring mistake to you will often pass unnoticed by them.

Remember that even if you are very nervous, *you will almost always look better than you feel*. Participants in my presentation skills programmes invariably underesti-mate their impact in trial presentations. When they watch a videotape of their efforts, they are often pleasantly surprised to find they look better than they had imagined.

The simplest way to free yourself from fear is to *focus primarily on your audience and their needs.* Excess nervousness and self-consciousness feed off each other in a vicious circle. When nervous, we tend to focus too much on ourselves and all our weaknesses; this negative focus creates more nervousness, and so on. Alternatively, if you keep your attention focused on the needs of your audience and on your commitment to fulfilling your objectives, you won't have time or cause to worry.

Finally, *most audiences have been habituated to a very low standard of presentation.* People are regularly exposed to lifeless, unimaginative presentations that seem

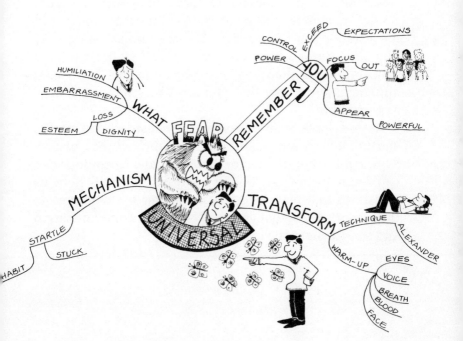

to drone on interminably. Because you care enough about excellence to have read this far, you will undoubtedly rise well above the average audience's expectations.

SUMMARY

In order to transform fear, you must first recognize that there is nothing wrong with feeling fear – it is a universal phenomenon. It is your reaction to fear that is important. Secondly, become familiar with the manifestations of the startle pattern, and begin to free yourself from it by studying the Alexander Technique and practising the Balanced Resting State. Thirdly, remember to warm up before every presentation. Use the warming-up exercises described in this chapter or make up your own. And finally, remember these comforting thoughts: your audience wants you to succeed; they are human beings like you; you are in a position of power and control; you are probably better than you think; focus primarily on your audience; and know that you are likely to exceed their expectations.

As we have seen through the consideration of the startle pattern, fear manifests itself through our bodies. Through the application of the Alexander Technique, we can learn to use our bodies in ways that will help us transform that fear. In the next chapter we will explore the powerful role that your body plays in communication and how to make the most of it.

CHAPTER 8

Let your body talk

He who knows that power is inborn ... and so perceiving, throws himself unhesitatingly on his thought, instantly rights himself, stands in the erect position, commands his limbs, works miracles.
Ralph Waldo Emerson

... let your own discretion be your tutor: suit the action to the word, the word to the action.
William Shakespeare

Your 'body language' – posture, movement, gesture, eye contact and voice – has tremendous impact on your audience. When you address a group of people, they are constantly responding, consciously and unconsciously, to what your body is 'saying' to them. Research shows that 55 per cent of your presentation's impact is determined by your posture, gestures and eye contact, 38 per cent by your voice tone and inflection, and only 7 per cent by the content of your presentation.[26]
Yet habit or fear leads many presenters to hide their

bodies behind podia or lecterns, becoming no more than 'talking heads' to their audiences. If you wish to communicate with maximum impact, you must emerge from behind the podium and discover how to make the most of your body language.

Distracting body language such as constricted posture, unconscious swaying movements, pencil fondling, averted eyes and frequent 'ums' and 'uhs' will interfere with the integrity of your communication. On the other hand, a relaxed, upright posture, a purposeful economy of movement, fluid gestures, lively eyes and an expressive voice will capture an audience's attention and greatly enhance the power of your message.

If your body language is not synchronized with your message, you lose credibility. In the words of the old Chinese proverb, 'Watch out for the man whose stomach doesn't move when he laughs.'

In this chapter, I will show you how to eliminate distracting, unnecessary elements of your body language, while making the most of what remains.

DEVELOPING ARTICULATE BODY LANGUAGE

In order to develop articulate body language, begin by understanding that all its main elements – posture, movement, gesture, eye contact and voice – are intimately related and interdependent. For example, if your posture is rigid, it leads to stiffness in your movement, tightness in your voice and restriction of your gestures. More than any particular element, *it is the overall coordination of the various components of your body language – with the message you are attempting to communicate – which is of primary importance.* However, in order to build this synchronization of body and message, we must begin by treating each of the elements of body language separately.

Posture. Your posture is the most fundamental statement you make with your body. An aligned, upright posture communicates a message of confidence and integrity. It says that you are 'together' and 'on the level'. Yet most people's posture is either collapsed, marked by a concave chest and slumping shoulders, or rigid, with a stiff neck and raised shoulders. What kind of message do these postures communicate?

An integrated body posture – one that will communicate positively to an audience – is balanced, upright and effortless.

I know of no better way to develop such a posture than to study the Alexander Technique, and to practise the Balanced Resting State explained on pages 66–8. One can also learn useful lessons from other disciplines, such as the martial arts, and various athletic activities in which participants cultivate a 'basic posture' as a point of departure for all movement.

In the same way, you should aim to develop a basic posture for presenting – a stance which will give you a solid grounding for all your body language.

The basic posture. Begin by practising the Balanced Resting State. Then, standing in front of a mirror, place your feet approximately shoulder-length apart. Rest your hands at your sides. Stand upright, with your shoulders resting easily on your torso. Imagine your back 'smiling' as you sense the floor supporting you. Use the mirror to give you feedback on your alignment, and your success in avoiding unnecessary, fidgeting movements. Practise standing quietly – without stiffening – for thirty seconds at a time. As you become comfortable with this basic stance, you can begin practising it while engaged in casual conversation.

This simple posture is incredibly powerful, as many actors who have worked years to master it will tell you. It projects confidence and power. Audiences become more receptive and responsive when you stand before them so calmly, and with such pure dignity.

Movement. With an integrated, basic posture as your point of departure, you are better able to realize your potential for communicating through movement.

Audiences are either distracted or attracted by all the movements that you make. Unnecessary, unconscious movements, such as swaying, rocking or pacing, will distract and annoy the audience. Awareness is the key to freeing yourself from these unnecessary movements, and is best cultivated by watching yourself on video (or in a large mirror if video is unavailable). As your awareness increases, so will your ability to leave out unwanted movements, and you will find it easier to move in a natural, expressive manner.

Moving in relaxed coordination with what you are saying not only engages your audience, but also prevents you from stiffening, as often happens when one sits or stands in one place for too long. Examples of natural, expressive movements might include walking towards your audience when emphasizing a point, or walking away, leaving them to contemplate a question you have just posed.

Make all your movements purposeful. If you are not sure of where or how to move, then return to your basic posture.

Gestures. Just as a conductor uses a baton to synchronize the orchestra, you can employ gestures to help conduct your message to the brains of your audience. When used appropriately, gestures provide another 'wavelength' upon which an audience can receive your communication.

Gestures can be tremendously powerful. To take full advantage of this power, it is essential that you *avoid unnecessary gestures*. An unnecessary gesture is one that does not aid you in communicating your message. Examples include habits such as pencil fondling, table tapping, hand wringing, hair curling, and hand-in-pocket change rattling.

If you wish to excel, your gestures must be natural, expressive and clear. Attempts to teach a particular set of gestures, however, are doomed to failure because the essence of effective gestural communication is spontaneity and authenticity. Gestures must emerge naturally from within the individual, rather than being imposed from the outside. When people are trained to use a particular pattern of gestures, they usually seem robotic, stilted and insincere.

In my presentation workshops, I help each student discover his or her own gestural vocabulary. One of my favourite examples concerns a manager of a large Swedish shipping company, who held his hands about four inches apart when describing his company's largest tanker. Being a shy man, to him this four-inch gesture probably felt big—a useful gestural description of a giant tanker. If he had been told the gesture was ludicrously small and urged to hold his hands wider apart, he would have felt uncomfortable, and given an even more stilted impression. I asked him to look at the video of his presentation to see if he was accurately depicting a big tanker. His immediate laughter showed that he recognized the insufficiency of his gesture. He tried again, making a gesture twice the size. Then he looked at the video, and saw that he still wasn't doing justice to the pride of his company's fleet. After a few more takes, he extended his hands fully, and his voice boomed: 'Ve haf really big tanker!', while his colleagues applauded wildly.

Develop your gestural vocabulary by experimenting with the following exercises that I use with my students. Do these in front of a mirror, or better still, a video camera.

Try different gestures to help you communicate each of the following phrases. Create your own context for each one. Say each phrase out loud as you make the gesture. And have fun!

Today I will be covering three major points.
We'll be developing this project from the ground up.
If you agree, please raise your hand.
Let's all stand up and have a stretch.
We sell the biggest system in the industry, for the smallest price.
She placed it sixteen inches down from the upper left-hand corner of the rear wall, next to the one he placed there yesterday.

Now for the advanced part of the exercise. Experiment with your gestures by reciting the following (remember to say each quote aloud):

- 'This is the true joy in life. The being used for a purpose, recognized by yourself as a mighty one; the being thoroughly worn out before you are thrown on the scrap heap; the being a force of nature instead of a feverish, selfish, little clod of ailments and grievances, complaining that the world will not devote itself to making you happy.' George Bernard Shaw

- 'No one who, like me, conjures up the most evil of those half tamed demons who inhabit the human breast, and seeks to wrestle with them, can expect to come through the struggle unscathed.' Sigmund Freud.

- 'Speak the speech, I pray you, as I pronounced it to you, trippingly on the tongue ... nor do not saw the air too much with your hand, thus, but use all gently; for in the very torrent, tempest, and, as I may say, the whirlwind of passion, you must acquire and beget a temperance that may give it smoothness ... be not too tame neither, but let your own discretion be your tutor, suit your action to the word, and your word to the action ...' William Shakespeare

In addition to practising the above exercise, which you can develop and expand on your own, take every opportunity to study gesture in everyday communication. Observe others, noticing the ratio between effective and unnecessary gestures. Watch television without the sound. Play charades. One of the best exercises is to observe, or better, study, the sign language used by deaf people. And finally, practise delivering your whole presentation without using any words at all!

Eye contact. Imagine that you are waiting to make a turn at a traffic light. The driver of a car in the next lane turns to make eye contact with you, indicating the desire to move in front of you. Your eyes meet. Do you let him in? The chances are that unless you're in a rotten mood, you do.

Eye contact is a humanizing element in an often impersonal world. It is a crucial aspect of communication, and thus an important part of every successful presentation.

Eye contact should be a simple, natural expression of your interest in the audience. It allows you also to monitor their level of interest and understanding of your message. Making eye contact with your audience draws their attention, helping them to feel more personally involved.

As I mentioned in the previous chapter, however, speakers often suffer under the delusion that their audience is an impersonal mass, and that eye contact with individuals is therefore impossible. The inability to make eye contact may also be caused by fear, lack of confidence, or simply thinking too much about oneself instead of the audience.

You can develop your innate ability to make contact and communicate with your eyes by experimenting in the following ways.

- Look in the mirror, and express these feelings and emotions using only your eyes: surprise, anger, scepticism, intrigue, intensity, love, confusion, confidence, irony, boredom, fear, playfulness, sincerity, wonder.

  If possible, practise this exercise with a friend, and let him or her guess which of the feelings is being communicated. Have fun making up additional material.

- Practise looking people in the eye in ordinary conversation. Experiment with holding the eye contact a little bit longer than usual. But remember, it is the quality of the contact that counts more than the duration.

- When you enter a room, particularly just before a presentation, look around and make eye contact with as many people as you can.

- While delivering your presentation, make regular eye contact with the friendliest-looking person on each side and in the middle of the room. This will help you become more comfortable with eye contact, and you will find it easier to make contact with other members of the audience. It will also help you to avoid being lured, by the friendly eyes of one person, into the common trap of directing your whole presentation to one part of the room.

- As your confidence builds, experiment with making regular eye contact with the unfriendliest-looking person on either side and in the middle of the room. See if you can draw them out with your eyes as you speak.

Perhaps more than any other element, eye contact reflects your interest in your audience, and determines your level of rapport with them.

Voice. Research shows that a major part of the impact of your presentation stems from the way you use your voice.[27] It is your primary tool of communication, and has the potential to be tremendously expressive. You can, with your voice alone, communicate many shades of meaning. Consider, for example, how much information can be gleaned from the tone of the first word spoken in a telephone conversation.

Your voice, like your posture, gestures, movements and eye contact, should be natural, expressive and clear. You can refine your voice by recognizing and eliminating unnecessary elements in your vocal usage. In order to do this, you must first learn how to pause.

Learn to pause. Great musicians have often stated that it is not so much the way in which a note is played, as the pauses between the notes, which create their art. So it is with the speaking voice.

Pausing is a natural part of speaking. Yet anxiety often causes speakers to fill their pauses with 'ums', 'ers', 'you knows' and other unnecessary, distracting noises. A powerful, expressive speaking rhythm is characterized by frequent, complete pauses. *Learning to pause appropriately is the single most important element in making the most of your voice.*

Pausing gives you the opportunity to think about what to say next, and to hear what you have just said. A pause gives you time to collect yourself and breathe fully. It also gives your audience time to assimilate your message, and feel more relaxed. Furthermore, an appropriate pause actually draws an audience's attention and interest.

In order to develop your ability to pause appropriately, you must first of all realize that *your audience welcomes the pause.* Secondly, don't be afraid to make your pause complete. Remember that the flow of adrenalin will tend to speed up your sense of time, so that a pause which may seem like an eternity to you is barely noticeable to the audience. Finally, experiment by speaking into a tape recorder, varying and extending your pauses, leaving out the ums and ers, and remembering to breathe. Then listen to your voice on the tape in order to develop your sense of when and how to pause.

Take your time. Many speakers talk too fast, often speeding up as their speech progresses. This can cause poor articulation, slurring or swallowing of words, and a loss of contact with the audience. Talking too fast usually occurs because of nervousness or over-excitement. Never allow yourself to be hurried as you speak, even if you are short on time. If you find that your time is running out, trim your less crucial content rather than talking faster. Whatever the cause, the best remedy for talking too fast is to pause regularly. Pausing allows you to breathe and collect yourself, and makes it much easier to take your time.

The great opera singer Nellie Melba once said that the voice can be used in three ways: it can be held in, forced out, or given to an audience easily and graciously. In addition to pausing, there are several other important considerations for learning to use your voice easily and graciously.

Use tone and inflection. Your voice is a naturally expressive instrument. The movement of tone and inflection gives your voice its expressive life; suppressing this natural movement results in monotony. Monotony is deadening – one of the surest ways to put your audience to sleep. It is a way of anaesthetizing oneself against fear, rather than facing it and using the heightened energy as an expressive force.

Another way in which people often interfere with natural expressiveness is to distort it through being phoney. Nervousness often causes speakers to 'posture' their voices in a constrained and artificial manner, leading them to try too hard to give a particular impression. The irony is that *trying* to sound authoritative, for example, communicates a lack of trust in one's own authority. Other common examples of phoniness include trying to sound nice, sincere or profound.

In many cases, distortion of the voice is caused or

perpetuated by excessive, chronic tension of the jaw. The jaw tends to be a centrepoint of stress for most people, and learning to free the jaw is a crucial element in liberating one's voice. The following exercises will help you increase your awareness of jaw tension and begin releasing it, thus enhancing your natural sense of tone and inflection.

- Begin by reading the following poem, exaggerating the tension in your jaw. Listen carefully to the quality of your voice while reading. Use a tape recorder if possible.

> *Thirty spokes are made one by holes in a hub,*
> *By vacancies joining them for a wheel's use;*
> *The use of clay in moulding pitchers*
> *Comes from the hollow of its absence;*
> *Doors, windows in a house,*
> *Are used for their emptiness;*
> *Thus we are helped by what is not,*
> *To use what is.*
>
> Laotze, *The Tao Te Tchng*

- Next, place your index finger in between your upper and lower molars on one side of your mouth for thirty seconds. Then allow your jaw to drop freely without the help of your finger for another thirty seconds. This will help you discover the natural drop of your jaw. When you first do this exercise, you will probably feel like an idiot. Practise regularly, until it feels comfortable and natural to release your jaw in this manner.

- Grasp your chin firmly, and gently waggle your jaw up and down for one minute. Be certain to move only your jaw, keeping your head still.

- Now read the poem again, and notice the difference in the quality of your voice.

The regular practise of these jaw release exercises will help your natural sense of tone and inflection to emerge. You can explore your vocal expressiveness further by experimenting with the following exercise.

Say 'hello', in a way which communicates each of the following feelings: surprise, anger, scepticism, intrigue, intensity, love, confusion, confidence, irony, boredom, fear, playfulness, sincerity, wonder.

Do the exercise again, this time using the phrase: 'The report is due on Tuesday.'

For the advanced part of the exercise, express *all* of the feelings listed above in one recitation of the following, from *King Lear*.

> Have more than thou showest,
> Speak less than thou knowest,
> Lend less than thou owest,
> Ride more than thou goest,
> Learn more than thou trowest,
> Set less than thou throwest ...
> And thou shalt have more
> Than two tens to a score.

Practise these exercises with a friend, and guess which of the feelings is being communicated. Enjoy making up additional material.

Develop volume control. In order to make full use of your expressive abilities, be certain that the audience can hear what you are saying. If you are not sure you can be heard (or if you think you are speaking too loudly), ask your audience for feedback, and modulate your volume accordingly.

Raising and lowering your voice appropriately is an essential aspect of effective speaking. It allows you greater scope for emphasizing your message, and enhances your expressiveness. You can use the following exercise to practise modulating your voice appropriately. Notice the effects of volume on your vocal expressiveness as you practise.

Read the following poem four times: in a whisper; in an ordinary conversational tone; as though you were speaking to a group of ten people; and then to a group of fifty people. Speak easily and graciously – don't strain your voice.

> *Awaken each clause with tender pause.*
> *Recite each section with tone and inflection;*
> *And speak each word so it can be heard!*
> Anonymous

In addition to practising the exercises given in this section, I also recommend that you develop greater flexibility and expressiveness in your voice by singing, learning other languages and by mimicking various accents.

BODY-MESSAGE SYNCHRONY

Having considered the elements of body language individually, now put them all together. Observe the effects of various gestures on your voice tone. Notice how your posture affects your movements and eye contact. Try any of the exercises above, and note the coordination between all the elements of your body language.

Of all the elements discussed in this chapter, posture is the most fundamental. A balanced, upright posture opens your voice, frees movement and gesture, and enhances alertness, thereby encouraging better eye contact. Remember, however, that when you are working on any of the elements of body language, you are working on them all.

Most importantly, be aware of the synchrony between the elements of body language and your message. When words say one thing and body language another, the result gives an impression of confusion, insincerity or deceit. In his debate with President Reagan, for example, Walter Mondale tried to capture his adversary's constituency by emphasizing a strong national defence. Mondale was clearly coached to use the word 'strength' frequently, and to pound his fist on the podium every time he said it. Unfortunately for the Democrats, Mondale's fist-pounding was weak and unconvincing, accompanied by a cracking in his voice and a slight aversion of his gaze. This inconsistency of body language and message was a key factor in his defeat by the 'Great Communicator'.

Politics and the television can provide many amusing opportunites for observing variations in the relationship between body language and message. The study of salespeople provides another. Salespeople are all too often characterized as crooked or beady-eyed. Interestingly, both of these terms refer to a fundamental lack of integrity expressed through their bodies. The finest salespeople know that the ultimate key to success is believing in themselves and their product, a belief which is communicated through the integrity of their body language.

The only way to ensure synchrony between your body

language and the message you are imparting is to be honest with yourself and your audience. There is no substitute for authenticity.

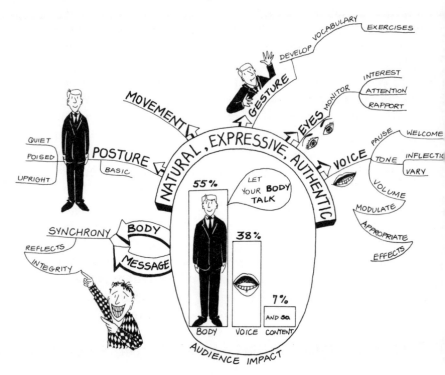

SUMMARY

The information and exercises in this chapter are designed to help you unleash your tremendous innate capacity for vibrant, powerful communication. A balanced, upright posture, dynamic movement, animated gestures, lively eyes and an expressive voice are all part of your birthright. As I have emphasized throughout this chapter, the key to gaining access to your natural expressiveness is to *leave out the unnecessary elements* that interfere with it. This will come with practise, experience, and a commitment to authenticity.

Michelangelo created some of his greatest sculptures by seeing the perfect form inside the stone. All the information and exercises in this book are designed to help you emerge fully and present yourself in the simplest, least artificial way possible. You now have all the tools you need to reach a peak of confidence and self-assurance.

Take the elements and put them all together.

Your audiences are waiting to see and hear you.

Put your best foot forward. PRESENT YOURSELF!

And in the next chapter, I'll give you some hints on how to continue your development as a presenter.

CHAPTER 9

Better and better

In order to succeed, double your failure rate.
Thomas Watson, President and founder of IBM

Just before he died, the great artist Auguste Renoir completed his final painting. His last words were: 'I think I'm beginning to understand something about [art].' Renoir possessed the essential quality which is characteristic of all true high performers – a lifelong commitment to learning.

The more knowledge and experience you have in a given area, the easier it becomes to learn more. At the same time, as your knowledge and experience increase, so does your awareness of the vast amount that remains to be learned. This is why the truly wise are always humble as well.

Whatever your current level as a presenter, there is a great deal more for you to learn, and unlimited potential for improvement. In order to tap your full potential, you must commit yourself to getting better and better, recognizing that you have the opportunity to improve every single time you make a presentation.

In this chapter there are some simple strategies which will help you continue your development as a high performance presenter.

THE ROAD TO EXCELLENCE

Feed your visualization of excellence. Think of yourself as a superior presenter, regularly building and refining your visualization of excellence. Be on the lookout for anything that can help you improve your presentations: observe other excellent presenters whenever possible; look for facts, stories, literary references, parables, audio-visuals – anything you can use to update and improve your material and delivery.

Take every opportunity to present. Practise at every possible opportunity; there is no substitute for experience. Tell stories and jokes to friends. Give informal talks to anyone who will listen. Join your local speakers' club, or take an evening class in public speaking.[28]

Seek feedback. Consider how a baby learns. It absorbs all the data it can with enthusiasm and wonder – instantly translating 'mistakes' into learning experiences, and thus learning at remarkable speed without losing self-confidence. Cultivate this same high performance learning attitude while seeking feedback on your presentations.

Do your best to discover what kind of impact you have on an audience. If appropriate, hand out evaluation forms, ask questions of audience members, or invite trusted friends or colleagues to attend your presentations for the purpose of giving you detailed feedback. An accurate critique is the greatest gift you can receive.

One of the finest ways of ensuring high-quality feedback is to set up a mutual arrangement with a trusted friend or colleague who shares your commitment to high performance. I personally have used this system over a period of more than twelve years with great success. Arrange to attend as many of each other's presentations as you possibly can, and to make comprehensive notes on one another's performances (you can use the presentations journal described on pages 95–7 as a guide for your notes).

Plan a time to meet and exchange feedback, and use the following procedure. Ask your partner to begin by focusing only on those aspects of your presentation which, in his opinion, could be improved. The feedback should be kept ruthlessly honest, objective and specific. When receiving your critique, take notes and don't explain or defend yourself. Ask questions only to gain further clarity. This form of listening allows you to get unusually pure feedback. Once the focus on your weaknesses has been completed (allow a maximum of fifteen minutes), do the same exercise – this time focusing on your strengths. Again, it is important to listen without responding in order to gain a full appreciation and understanding of what you did well.

This exercise is tremendously powerful and if you practise it faithfully, with a perceptive and sensitive partner, it will lead you to insights about your presentations that would otherwise be impossible to gain. As you develop skill in criticizing your partner's presentation, so will your own model of excellence grow.

Keep a presentations journal. Create a journal to help

you plan and evaluate your presentations. Use this to record information about the audience, your objectives, the environment and your content before you give your talk. After each presentation, evaluate objectively your strengths and weaknesses, and record them. You can use the following questions and format as a guide for building your own comprehensive high performance presentations journal. Reviewing your journal regularly will help you to hone your high performance attitude and speed your progress.

PRESENTATIONS JOURNAL

A Preparation
Use this section in preparing for your presentation, then afterwards review it and add your comments. You may include:

- A Mind Map of your presentation
- Key facts about the audience (number of people, expectations, gender, etc.)
- Objectives for this presentation
- Possible questions or objections from the audience
- Starting time
  Finishing time
- Arranging the introduction
- Logistics
- Completing the environmental checklist

Checklist	*Comments*
.... Lighting	....
.... Air quality and temperature	....
.... Furniture	....
.... Microphone	....
.... AV equipment	....
.... Music	....
.... NO SMOKING signs	....
.... Plants	....
.... Flowers	....
.... Acoustics	....
.... Miscellaneous	....

- *Warming up exercises (space and time arranged?)*

B Feedback

Record your comments and, where appropriate, rate
yourself in each area on a scale of 1 to 10.

- *Objectives accomplished*   1 2 3 4 5 6 7 8 9 10

  Comments:

- Use of audio-visuals   1 2 3 4 5 6 7 8 9 10

  Comments:

- *Posture*   1 2 3 4 5 6 7 8 9 10

  Comments:

- *Gestures*   1 2 3 4 5 6 7 8 9 10

  Comments:

- *Movements*   1 2 3 4 5 6 7 8 9 10

  Comments:

- *Voice*   1 2 3 4 5 6 7 8 9 10

  Comments:

- *Overall body language*   1 2 3 4 5 6 7 8 9 10

  Comments:

- *Major weaknesses of my presentation:*

- *Major strengths:*

- *What would I do differently next time?*

- My own comfort and enjoyment level:

- General comments:

Keep your journal in a special file along with your Mind Maps and any evaluation forms you receive. Even if you don't record this information, you can still benefit by asking yourself the journal questions after each presentation.

There is one other essential point which has been implicit throughout this book: the key to giving great presentations is having fun. So practise, enjoy and have fun.

CHAPTER 10

20 Questions and answers

When I lead seminars on presentation skills, the participants always ask me excellent questions. Since you may
have similar questions after reading *Present Yourself*, I'd
like to try to anticipate, and answer, some of them here.

1. **The organization where I work is very conservative –
   and some of your suggestions on how I can make my
   presentations more creative may be too controversial
   for my superiors and co-workers. Under these circumstances, how can I make presentations better?**
   Balance your creativity with logic and sensitivity to your
   organization's culture. Gauge your organization's 'comfort zone' objectively – not from a position of fear, which
   will cause you to underestimate their receptivity to new
   ideas. Then try to work within and gently stretch this
   comfort zone. You don't have to be P. T. Barnum to give
   superior presentations. Just recall what makes people – in
   any context – pay attention and remember, and present
   yourself accordingly.

2. How much time should I give myself to rehearse a presentation thoroughly?

There is no set minimum or maximum amount of time – rehearse until you are confident. Set your objectives, then generate, organize and become comfortable with your material, as soon as you can. This will give you more time to experiment with creative ways to deliver your message.

3. What if I have to give a presentation at very short notice?

In order to succeed under pressure, you must maintain your poise and act confidently. You must not allow yourself to be undermined by fear. It is essential that you begin immediately to visualize a successful outcome. Use Mind Mapping to generate ideas and organize your content and objectives, then practise the Mind Map memory method.

4. If I have to give many presentations in a short space of time, how do I prevent burn-out?

Be sensitive to your own energy level. The excitement and rush of adrenalin following successful presentations can obscure your awareness of your own exhaustion. It takes a lot of energy to give effective presentations. If you are on a busy speaking schedule, you must take good care of yourself to prevent burning out. Just like other performance professionals (athletes, actors, dancers, etc.), you must you sleep well, exercise regularly, and eat a healthy, balanced diet. I cannot overemphasize the importance of these three elements.

It is also essential that you take regular breaks, even in the midst of a demanding schedule. When you are speaking to groups day after day, you must give yourself regular periods of absolute quiet. Make a point of finding a time when you won't have to talk to anyone. This will not only help to save your voice, it may also save your sanity. And, when you give your audience a break during sessions, don't always stay around to answer questions – leave the room, and take a quiet, rejuvenating walk.

5. How do I maintain my enthusiasm when I have to give the same presentation repeatedly?

Every presentation is a learning opportunity for you. Take advantage of that fact, and you will never be bored. Also, remember that it is the first time for your audience. Think of them . . .

6. What should I remember in making presentations to people more senior than I?

Remember that you have been invited to address them for a reason. Take charge and present yourself with confidence. Generally, the more senior people are, the better they respond to those who conduct themselves in an authoritative manner. Never apologize for being there. Make sure that you dress immaculately and, if necessary, visualize how everyone in your audience looked in their first-form class photos!

7. If for some reason beyond my control I am confronted with an unfavourable environment (too hot, stuffy, poor lighting, etc.) for my presentation, what can I do to make the best of the situation?

If the environment is unfavourable, and there is nothing you can do to change it, acknowledge this in a light-hearted way and give your group more frequent breaks.

8. Do you have any advice about how to make presentations to children?

Treat them in the same way you would an adult audience – with respect. Children will probably need more frequent breaks in order to exorcize their abundant physical energy. Get them involved and active whenever possible. Keep your language simple, and remember that, just like adults, their brains will respond to colour, imagery and metaphor, so apply these elements liberally.

9. What should I do if I draw a blank in the middle of my presentation?

If you have prepared thoroughly for your presentation, you won't experience this very often. However, even the best prepared presenters occasionally experience a sudden loss of place, or a mental block. Your strength will lie in how you handle the situation. When you recognize that you have lost your place, *pause for a moment*, breathe deeply and collect yourself. If your train of thought does not immediately return, you can simply ask your audience, 'Where was I?' - at which point someone in the group will undoubtedly respond. This kind of honesty and directness will enhance your rapport with the audience.

10. What are the most common mistakes presenters make?

Not preparing thoroughly. Forgetting about the audience. Not giving enough breaks. Going on too long. Hiding behind audio-visuals. Apologizing. Speaking in a monotone. And, most importantly, under-estimating themselves.

11. Do you have any special advice for presenting on television?

Remember that when you look into a television camera, and speak to millions of people, you are speaking to millions of *individuals*. Talk as though you were speaking directly to any one of them. Exaggerate your gestures, and don't worry about coming on too strong.

12. How can I handle difficult people?

Most difficult people are difficult because they have a problem. Often it has nothing to do with you and your presentation. Some people are insecure and like to show off their knowledge, others may just have got out of bed on the wrong side that day. A few may actually be reacting to some aspect of your presentation. These problems can manifest themselves in anything from noisy paper shuffling to unnecessary or hostile questions. The best way to address such situations is, first of all, not to take them personally. Try to determine what the real issue is, and deal with it if possible.

When handling aggressive questions, listen carefully and find something in what the questioner is saying that you can agree with; avoid getting defensive. The better you are at empathizing, the easier it will be to defuse the situation. Don't let yourself get caught in a battle, even if you are sure you can overwhelm your 'opponent' with superior knowledge. You may win the battle, but lose your audience. If you maintain your rapport with the audience, you will find that they will be effectively self-policing, not tolerating significant disruption by a disgruntled member.

Finally, bear in mind that if you are well prepared and present yourself with confidence and authority, these kind of problems will rarely arise.

13. Can you give me some guidance on answering questions?

Always listen carefully for the essence of what is being asked, and treat every question with respect. Make sure that the question is heard by everyone, and repeat it if necessary. It is a good idea to pause and think about the question before answering. Answer concisely. If you do not know the answer, you can refer the question to the group. This is often a good idea even when you do know, as it encourages group involvement. Otherwise say, 'I don't know', with authority, and offer to seek the answer and provide it at some future time.

14. Is it possible to be a high performance presenter if I am physically disabled?

Certainly it is. Your honesty, integrity and willingness to reach out to your audience will determine your success.

15. Can you give some guidance on making sales presentations?

Be very clear about your own objectives. Know your audience – do they have the power to make the decision you want them to make? Know what they want and need, and give it to them. Be sensitive to the moment when your audience is 'sold', and don't go on beyond that point. Instead, ask for the sale.

16. Is it possible to apply a high performance approach in schools?

Absolutely. The best teachers have always intuitively practised this approach by combining logic and discipline with imagination and fun. One of my favourite examples of this concerns the winner of a Teacher of the

Year Award in America, whom I once saw on the television news. Her class was studying the Salem Witch Trials, and the interview began with the teacher screaming into the room on a skateboard, dressed in a pointed black hat, cackling wildly. The children in her class were all dressed in period costumes, and were absorbed in acting out scenes from the trial. The interviewer asked the children a number of challenging questions about the trials, which they all answered effortlessly and correctly. She asked the children if they enjoyed this class, and the answer was a resounding, 'It's the best class we've ever had!' As the interview progressed, the children were asked if they thought their teacher was strict, and they replied that she was the strictest, fairest and most demanding in the school.

The children were learning a tremendous amount, loved their teacher, and were having fun. The high performance approach balances logic and imagination, discipline and fun. This is what education should be!

17. How should I use humour?

Humour can be a marvellous tool for defusing stressful situations, relaxing yourself and your audience, and for helping people to remember what you have said. Spontaneous humour works best, so avoid 'canned' jokes and instead cultivate an appropriate light-heartedness.

18. How can I learn more about the Alexander Technique?

The Alexander Technique is best learned through individual lessons with a qualified teacher. Lessons usually last from thirty to forty-five minutes. Most teachers recommend a basic course of at least thirty lessons.

To find a qualified Alexander teacher in the United

Kingdom write to: The Society of Teachers of the Alexander Technique, 10 London House, 266 Fulham Road, London SW10.

19. What are some other applications of Mind Mapping?
Mind Mapping has hundreds of practical applications. Some of my favourites include planning vacations, parties, schedules and meetings; recording lectures, dreams, phone calls and study material; generating ideas for poetry and other creative work; solving problems; and resolving conflicts. Last but not least, Mind Maps are tremendously valuable tools for generating and organizing material for writing – articles, reports, books, etc.

Beyond its value in improving your productivity, Mind Mapping helps you to develop a balance between your logical and imaginative thinking capacities, thereby enhancing your mental flexibility and overall creativity.

20. Will developing a high performance approach to presenting affect other aspects of my life?
My experience shows that learning to present yourself is a tremendously powerful vehicle for self-development. In order fundamentally to improve your ability to express yourself to a group, you must grow as a human being. Be prepared to face your fears, insecurities and limiting habit patterns. You must learn to place your ego on the shelf as you actively seek feedback on your performance.

As you meet these challenges, you will gain valuable insights into your own nature and that of others. These insights will help you develop your skills in leadership and personal relationships, and will ultimately enhance your sense of self-confidence, poise and personal power.

Notes

1. Tony Buzan – personal communication. See also *The Brain User's Guide* (E.P. Dutton, New York, 1986). Buzan makes this assertion based on his assessment of the increase in the number of scientific papers published on the brain.

2. Wallace and Wallechinsky, *The Book of Lists* (William Morrow and Company, New York, 1977), p.469. Fear of public speaking is rated the number one fear of 4 per cent of the population in this survey, surpassing nuclear war, death, and financial ruin.

3. Tony Buzan, *Use Both Sides of Your Brain* (E.P. Dutton, New York, 1985). See the chapter entitled 'Your Mind Is Better Than You Think'.

4. Peter Russell, *The Brain Book* (Routledge and Kegan Paul, London, 1979). Note the discussion in Chapter 12, 'Is Everything Remembered?'

5. *Ibid.*, p.7. Russell states that we probably use even less than 1 per cent of our brains' potential; in his words, 'more likely .01 per cent or less!'

6. *Ibid.* Note the discussion in Chapter 4, 'The Two Sides of the Brain'. Since Sperry's original discoveries about the two sides of the brain, there has been a tremendous explosion of interest in this area. Researchers have found that each hemisphere is actually capable of doing the work of the other, and that the division of function is not as clear as it first seemed. I recommend thinking of the terms 'left-brained' and 'right-brained' as references to the skills of logic and imagination, respectively. Wherever these abilities may be 'located', our highest functioning results from their balanced use.

7. *Ibid.* Note the discussion in Chapter 8, 'Imagery And Its Relationship To Memory'.

8. Tony Buzan, *Use Both Sides of Your Brain*, op. cit. Note the discussion in Chapter 4, 'Noting'.

9. Betty Edwards, *Drawing on the Right Side of the Brain* (J.P. Tarcher, Los Angeles, 1979). A brilliant exposition of the 'brain benefits' of drawing.

10. Tony Buzan, *Use Both Sides of Your Brain*, op. cit. Note the discussion in Chapter 4, 'Noting'. See also Howe and Godfrey, *Student Note Taking as an Aid to Learning* (Exeter University, 1977).

11. Peter Russell, *The Brain Book*, op. cit. See Chapter 6, 'The Psychology of Memory'.

12. Christopher Turk, *Effective Speaking: Communicating in Speech* (E. & F.N. Spon, New York, 1985), p.49. Turk states 'the listeners must be able to grasp the structure of the talk. Make sure that you make the overall pattern of your presentation plain to the audience.'

13. *Ibid.*, p.75

14. Peter Russell, *The Brain Book*, op. cit. See Chapter 6, 'The Psychology of Memory'.

15. *Ibid.*

16. A. Richardson, *Mental Imagery* (Routledge and Kegan Paul, London, 1969), p.56.

17. Peter Russell, *The Brain Book*, op. cit. See Chapter 15.

18. I recommend the relaxation exercise taught in Dr Herbert Benson's book, *The Relaxation Response* (Collins, London, 1976).

19. John Basmajian, 'Conscious Control of Single Nerve Cells', *New Scientist*, December 1963, p.663.

20. John Diamond, *Behavioural Kinesiology: the new science for positive health through muscle testing* (Harper and Row, New York, 1979), pp.78-9.

21. Peter Russell, *The Brain Book*, op. cit., p.208.

22. John Diamond, *Behavioural Kinesiology*, op. cit. Note the discussion in Chapter 9, 'The Music in Your Life'.

23. Frank Pierce Jones, *Body Awareness in Action, A Study of the Alexander Technique* (Schocken Books, New York, 1976).

24. F.M. Alexander, *The Use of the Self* (reprinted by Centerline Press, CA, 1986).

25. This subtle form of manual guidance is unique and has to be experienced to be understood and appreciated.

26. Albert Mehrabian, *Silent Messages* (Wadsworth, England, 1971). See also M. Argyle *et al.*, 'The Communication of Superior and Inferior Attitudes by Verbal and Non-Verbal Signals', *British Journal of Social and Clinical Psychology*, Vol. 9 (1970), pp.222-31.

27. *Ibid*.

28. To obtain the address of your local club, contact the Association of Speakers' Clubs, 16 Rowanbank, Scone, Perthshire, PH2 6PU.

Suggested further reading

Alexander, F. Matthias, *The Use of the Self*, reprinted by Centerline Press, CA, 1986. The author's fascinating account of his discovery of the Alexander Technique.

Baker, Elsworth F., *Man in the Trap: The causes of blocked sexual energy* (Collier Books, New York, 1967). An incisive look at the work of Wilhelm Reich. Baker's book elaborates, with numerous examples, Reich's discoveries of various styles of 'character armour', the study of which offers profound insights for any student of presentation skills.

Bandler, Richard, and Grinder, John, *Frogs into Princes: Neuro Linguistic Programming* (Real People Press, Utah, 1979). A valuable introductory work on the subject of neuro-linguistic programming, a discipline which explores the fine points of non-verbal communication as well as different strategies of listening and learning.

Benson, Herbert, *The Relaxation Response* (Collins, London, 1976). The result of Benson's distillation of a pot-pourri of relaxation techniques into one simple, practical method, which can actually be learned from the book.

The Brain-Mind Bulletin, ed. Marylin Ferguson (Interface Press, CA). This bulletin offers well-written abstracts on the latest advances in brain studies. I particularly recommend their reprints on left/right-brain research.

Buzan, Tony, *Use Both Sides of Your Brain* (E. P. Dutton, New York, 1985). Buzan's classic work, originally published in 1971, established him as the father of 'whole-brain' education. This book is an invaluable guide for anyone interested in learning how to learn and communicate.

Buzan, Tony, *Use Your Memory* (BBC Publications, London, 1986). The best of the 'how-to' memory books. Buzan deals with the subject comprehensively; his techniques are easy to learn and immediately applicable.

Diamond, John, *Behavioural Kinesiology: the new science for positive health through muscle testing* (Harper and Row, New York, 1979). Diamond is a pioneer in the study of the subtle but powerful effects of various environmental factors, such as lighting and music, on audiences.

Dobson, Terry, and Miller, Victor, *Attactics: Giving in to Get Your Way* (Delacorte Press, New York, 1978). This book demonstrates a variety of creative strategies for dealing with conflict in everyday life. It is particularly valuable for the presenter interested in learning how to handle 'difficult people'.

Edwards, Betty, *Drawing on the Right Side of the Brain* (J. P. Tarcher, Los Angeles, 1979). Betty Edwards's book has become a classic in the field of whole-brain education. In addition to actually learning how to draw, the careful reader will also gain valuable insights into the role of imagery in thinking and creating.

Gardner, Howard, *Frames of Mind: The Theory of Multiple Intelligences* (Basic Books, New York, 1985). Gardner's book elaborates on seven major types of intelligences, and provides a useful perspective on the various styles of learning and listening.

Gelb, Michael, *Body Learning: An Introduction to the Alexander Technique* (Aurum Press, London, new ed. 1987). *Publishers Weekly* called this the most lucid book on the subject.

Hart, Leslie, *How the Brain Works* (Basic Books, New York, 1975). Hart provides a fascinating look at the workings of the human brain, emphasizing particularly its active, pattern-seeking nature. Very helpful in understanding the nature of audience recall.

Herrigel, Eugen, *Zen and the Art of Archery* (Vintage, New York, 1971). This delightful little book offers penetrating insights into the attainment of excellence in any discipline.

Jones, Frank Pierce, *Body Awareness in Action, A Study of the Alexander Technique* (Schocken Books, New York, 1976). This excellent book includes an extensive discussion of Jones's ground-breaking scientific study of the Alexander Technique, including his work on the startle pattern.

Peters, Tom, and Austin, Nancy, *A Passion for Excellence*

(Warner Books, New York, 1986). A valuable presentation of various corporate 'models of excellence'. This book repeatedly demonstrates the intimate relationship between leadership and effective presentation skills. The section on coaching has particular relevance for those who wish to develop a team approach to improving presentation skills.

Restak, Richard M., *The Brain: The Last Frontier* (Warner Books, New York, 1979). A thorough, easy to read discussion of brain science.

Rowse, A. L., *The Annotated Shakespeare* (Greenwich House, Crown Books, New York, 1984). Shakespeare's works provide the ultimate guide to presentation skills.

Russell, Peter, *The Brain Book* (Routledge and Kegan Paul, London, 1979). This superb text provides the research details behind Buzan's classic *Use Both Sides of Your Brain*.

Samuels, M., and Samuels, N., *Seeing With the Mind's Eye* (Random House, New York, 1976). This comprehensive work provides fascinating information on the history and uses of visualization.

Selye, Hans, *The Stress of Life* (McGraw Hill, New York, 1978). This is the original work on stress which introduced the notion of 'fight or flight'.

Turk, Christopher, *Effective Speaking: Communicating in Speech* (E. & F. N. Spon, New York, 1985). Turk's book is a very well researched, detailed guide to presentation skills. It is, however, unnecessarily limited by its focus on attaining only 'a decent standard of ordinary competence' rather than encouraging its readers to strive for excellence.

For further information on lectures, seminars and consulting services, contact:

High Performance Learning Center
4613 Davenport Street, N.W.
Washington, DC 20016, USA
(0101 202) 537 0775